Quilts
from the American
Homefront

121 Quilt Blocks Inspired by
Letters from World War II

Rosemary Youngs

CINCINNATI, OHIO

www.fwmedia.com

16 15 · 14 13 12   5 4 3 2 1

DISTRIBUTED IN CANADA BY FRASER DIRECT
100 Armstrong Avenue
Georgetown, ON, Canada L7G 5S4
Tel: (905) 877-4411

DISTRIBUTED IN THE U.K. AND EUROPE BY F+W MEDIA
INTERNATIONAL
Brunel House, Newton Abbot, Devon, TQ12 4PU, England
Tel: (+44) 1626 323200, Fax: (+44) 1626 323319
Email: postmaster@davidandcharles.co.uk

DISTRIBUTED IN AUSTRALIA BY CAPRICORN LINK
P.O. Box 704, S. Windsor NSW, 2756 Australia
Tel: (02) 4577-3555

Library of Congress Cataloging in Publication Data
Youngs, Rosemary
  Quilts from the American Homefront / by Rosemary Youngs.-- 1st ed.
    p. cm.
  Includes index.
  ISBN-13: 978-1-4402-3199-5 (alk. paper)
  1. Textile fabrics. 2. Dressmaking. 3. Sewing. I. Title.
  ND2300.W37 2006
  751.42'24343--dc22   2005020563

SRN: V7975
ISBN-13: 978-1-4402-3199-5

Editor: Layne Vanover
Desk Editor: Noel Rivera
Designer: Jodie Lystor
Production Coordinator: Greg Nock
Photographer: Stacey Clack

Dedication

It is with a heart full of love that I dedicate this book to my loving family. I love you more than words can ever express. You bless my life every day.

A Father Honored

Edward F. Sluja, the author's father, served in the United States Army during World War II.

Acknowledgements

Thank you so much to my dear husband Tom and our wonderful children: Stacey and her husband Micah, John and his wife Sarah, Amy and her husband Matt, and Jeff. Thanks also to my grand-children Hailey, Sophia and Dylan for all their love and support.

Thank you to my special friends, especially my women's Bible study at Trinity Reformed Church. I sincerely appreciate your companionship, your encouragement, your prayers and your confidence in me.

Thank you to all my wonderful quilting and nonquilting friends who are such a special part of my life; we are stitched together by our friendship. Thank you to the donut girls, the dear Jane group, my wonderful penpals and the Internet quilting groups.

To all the quilters who have inspired me along my journey, whether I have met you at a quilt shop, a retreat, at Beaver Island, Paducah or Shipshewana, thank you so much for your inspiration and friendship.

Thank you to Tammy Finkler for her beautiful machine quilting expertise and her willingness to fit my quilting projects into her schedule.

Thank you to my wonderful quilting friends who helped me make blocks for this quilt: Barbara Perrin, Gay Bomers, Elaine Frey, Patty Harrants, Carla Jolman, Connie Makl, Jeanne Meddaugh, Janis Nelson and Karen Weilder.

Thank you to my daughter, Stacey Clack, for her willingness to take the beautiful photographs used in this book.

I am indebted to the families represented in this book and to all of those who helped me with my research. A special thanks to those who have treasured the World War II letters of their ancestors and have preserved their stories.

Thank you to Electric Quilt Company for your willingness to help me with my projects and CDs.

Thank you also to Krause Publications for their confidence and encouragement during the writing of this book, especially managing editor Vanessa Lyman and acquisitions editor Christine Doyle. Thanks also to my book editor, Layne Vanover, for her work on the project.

Most importantly, I would like to thank God for the wonderful opportunities and people I have met through writing, and for always taking the pieces of my life, stitching them together and making something beautiful.

A World War II sewing kit issued by Great Falls Beer.

Table of Contents

Introduction

Even though World War II was fought overseas, the daily lives of those who lived here in the States were affected. Everyone on the homefront became involved and committed to doing his or her part—it was a time of great patriotism in this country.

One of the most invaluable ways to communicate with soldiers overseas was through letter writing. Families used written correspondence not only to keep in touch with loved ones, but to share important news from the homefront. For example, through letters, a soldier might learn he had become a new father or that he had lost a family member. As such, letters were cherished by many who served.

Seven sets of letters are featured in this book, giving an insight into the lives of those who served this country during World War II. It has been an honor for me to collect these treasures and to reunite the families with letters most of them never knew existed.

D-Cady and Katharine Herrick II

D-Cady Herrick II wrote his letters home to his wife Katharine. D-Cady enlisted in the United States Navy about a year after they were married. The Herrick family letters are in the author's collection. The photographs were used with permission from D-Cady Herrick III.

Everett Allen and Mary Elizabeth Tucker

Everett reported for training at the Great Lakes training center and later was stationed on the *USS Ajax*. He wrote his letters home to his wife Mary. The Tucker family letters and photographs were used with permission from their son, Chris L. Tucker.

Clarence and Floy Falstrom

Clarence served as a corporal in the Signal Corps in the United States Army. He wrote his letters home to his wife Floy on small note cards. The Falstrom family letters are in the author's collection. The photographs were used with permission from his niece, the Chris and Joan Tucker family.

Marie Booker and Wyndom L. Brown

Marie Booker began writing letters to Wyndom Brown, who was serving in the United States Army during World War II. Marie was still in school when she wrote her letters to Wyndom. The Booker family letters and photographs are in the author's collection.

Carter O. Lilly and Genny N. Brun

Genny met Carter in a park when he was on a furlough. Carter started writing Genny letters in 1942. The letters from Carter O. Lilly are in the author's collection. The photographs are used with permission from Genny's sister, Lillian.

Robert Paul DeWalt

Robert Paul DeWalt served in the United States Army Air Corps and was sent to New Guinea during World War II. He wrote his letters home to his mother. The letters and photographs are used with permission from his daughter, Gladys E. DeWalt Berger.

Stephen C. Dvorak

Stephen C. Dvorak left home to enroll at the Webb Institute of Naval Architecture, then later left the Webb Institute to join the United States Army as a technician. The letters featured are from his mother to Stephen. The letters are in the author's collection. Photographs are used with permission from Stephen's niece, Carolyn Yates.

How to Use This Book

Embark on an historical journey through the lives of individuals who wrote and received letters during World War II, as you enjoy piecing together quilt blocks inspired by their correspondence.

This book is divided into two sections. Though brief, the first section is crucial in helping you create your World War II quilt. Here, you will find general instructions and techniques, as well as a list of fabrics and supplies that you will need. The second section makes up the bulk of the book and contains a brief introduction to each set of World War II correspondents, the letters themselves, and all 121 full-size block patterns.

Fabrics, Tools and Supplies

Fabrics

Choosing fabrics is one of my favorite aspects of quilt making, as well as an important part of creating a successful finished piece. Due to the small size of the blocks, selecting fabrics that have small-scale prints will be more effective than using those with large-scale prints. Also, be sure to choose a variety of background fabrics and lattice fabrics to make your finished quilt visually interesting.

Thread

I recommend a 100 percent cotton, 50-weight thread for sewing the pieces of your blocks together. It resists shrinking and is available in a variety of colors. I use the same thread for appliqué, though sometimes I substitute a silk thread. For hand quilting, I recommend a strong 100 percent cotton thread.

Scissors

I keep two different pairs of scissors on hand —one for fabric and one for paper.

Rotary Cutters, Rulers and Mat

I keep two rotary cutters on hand—one to cut fabrics and the other to cut through the fabric once it is sewn to the foundation paper.

Sewing Machine Needle

It is very important to use a size 14 sewing machine needle if you are foundation piecing the blocks together; this makes it much easier to rip off the foundation paper.

Foundation Paper

Use a lightweight paper that is not only easy to tear away but easy to trace on. Try different papers such as newsprint, computer paper, or even tracing paper to find what works best for you. Remember to choose a paper that can run easily through a copy machine.

Piecing the Blocks

This book contains 121 patterns. Trace the pattern onto your medium of choice, then cut it out to make a template. Once cut out, templates can be used in either hand or machine piecing. The more accurate you are in tracing your templates, the better your blocks will fit together.

Pieced Block and Appliqué Templates

I prefer to use freezer paper, not only because you can easily see through it to trace the template, but also because the template can be used several times.

1. Place freezer paper over the drawing of the block in your book. Using a pencil with thin lead, trace all the shapes onto the freezer paper, adding a ¼" seam allowance on all sides. Number the pieces to keep them in order.
2. Iron the freezer paper onto the right side of your fabric. Remember to set your iron to a no-steam setting.
3. Cut out all the shapes and assemble as shown on the pattern.

Foundation Piecing Instructions

Foundation piecing is an easy technique for piecing blocks. In this method, fabric is sewn to the paper foundation following a numerical sequence.

1. Decide how many units the pattern will be divided into.
2. Trace the pattern onto the foundation paper using a ruler and thin-lead pencil. Copy all of the lines of each unit, and add a ¼" seam allowance around each unit.

3. Number the foundation paper in the order that the pieces should be sewn together.
4. Position the fabrics right sides together on the unmarked side of the foundation paper.
5. Stitch on the sewing line between the numbers using a very small stitch (1.5 on most machines).
6. Continue stitching all pieces in numerical order until the block or unit is complete. Trim the fabric so that it is even with the outside line of the foundation. If you have more than one unit for a block, match the units and stitch them together.
7. Keep the foundation papers in place for now; it will help to stabilize the blocks when you sew them together with your lattice.

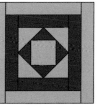

Some blocks can be pieced together as a whole unit.

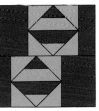

Some blocks need to be pieced together in separate units and then stitched together to make the whole unit.

Assembling the Quilt

Materials
- 3¼ yd. fabric for the outer border
- 2¾ yd. fabric for the inner border
- 5–6 1 yd. pieces of various prints for the lattice and background
- ½ yd. fabric for the cornerstones
- 1 yd. fabric for the binding
- 9¾ yd. backing fabric
- Various fat quarters of coordinating fabrics for the blocks

Cutting Instructions
From the lattice and cornerstone fabric, cut:
- 144 cornerstones (2" × 2")
- 264 lattice strips (2" × 6")

From the inner border fabric, cut lengthwise:
- 2 inner border strips (3½" × 84½")
- 2 inner border strips (3½" × 90½")

From the outer border fabric, cut lengthwise:
- 2 outer border strips (8½" × 90½")
- 2 outer border strips (8½" × 106½")

From the binding fabric, cut:
- 11 strips (2½" wide by the width of your fabric)

From the backing fabric, cut:
- 3 pieces of fabric 3¼ yds. long

Assembling the Quilt Top
1. Sew the blocks into 11 rows of 11 blocks each with a lattice strip between each block. Each row should have 11 blocks and 12 vertical lattice strips.

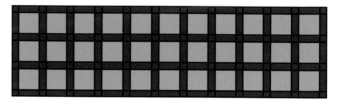

2. Sew the 12 joining rows, which will consist of 12 cornerstones and 11 lattice strips. Sew the rows together, matching the seams of the cornerstones with the seams of the lattice strips. When all 11 rows are assembled, your project should measure 84½" × 84½".

3. Sew the two inner border strips (3½" × 84½") to the top and bottom. Next, add the remaining two border strips (3½" × 90½") to the sides.

4. Sew the outer border strip (8½" × 90½") to the sides. Next, add the remaining two outer border strips (8½" × 106½") to the top and bottom.

Add the Backing
1. Trim the selvage of each of the three pieces of backing fabric ¼" past the selvage.

2. Sew the pieces together to form a rectangle measuring approximately 114" × 114". Press the seams open.

3. Lay the backing right side down on the floor or table. Secure it with tape so that it will remain flat and taut.

4. Center the batting and quilt top right side up. Thread or pin baste the top together.

5. If desired, trim some of the batting and backing off of the quilt. Leave approximately 4" around the edges of the quilt top.

6. Quilt as desired.

Binding the Quilt

1. Sew the 11 binding strips together into 1 long strip.

2. Iron the binding in half, wrong sides together, along the length of the whole strip.

3. Lay the binding in the middle of one side of the finished quilt and stitch a ¼" seam, with your raw edges facing the edge of your quilt. Leave 3–4" on the end to join the bias later.

4. Sew within ¼" of the edge of the first corner. With the needle in the down position, turn the quilt, and backstitch off the edge.

5. Fold the binding strip up, away from the corner, to make a 45-degree fold.

6. Bring the strip straight up and align it with the raw edge of the next side.

7. Sew within ¼" of the next corner. Repeat until you approach your starting point.

8. As you get to the point where you first started stitching, stop and overlap both loose ends of the binding where they meet on the quilt.

9. Stitch right sides together, using a ¼" seam allowance.

10. Turn the binding over to the back. Using a blind stitch, sew the binding down on the stitching line.

Alternative Quilt Templates

If you don't want to make the full-size World War II quilt using all 121 blocks, try one of these smaller projects. I've included patterns for a table runner, a small wall hanging, a crib-size quilt and a twin-size quilt. Regardless your choice of project, you'll create a quilt that will be treasured for generations to come!

Table Runner
17" × 32"

Small Wall Hanging

32" × 32"

Crib Quilt
39½" × 47"

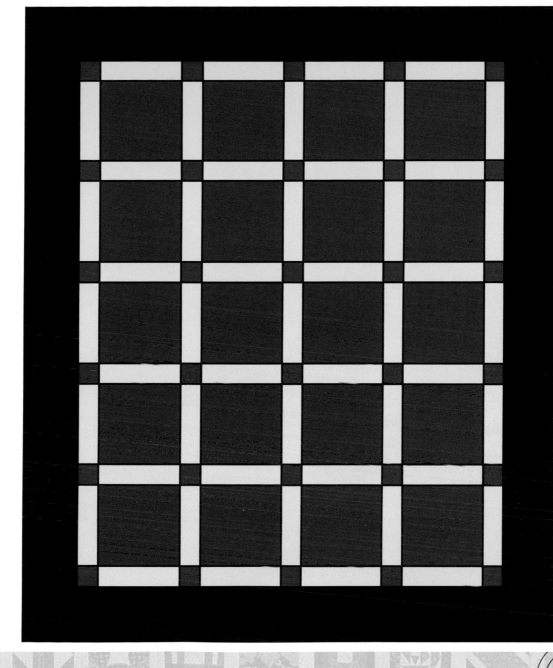

Twin Quilt
65" × 96"

World War II Quilt

106" × 106"

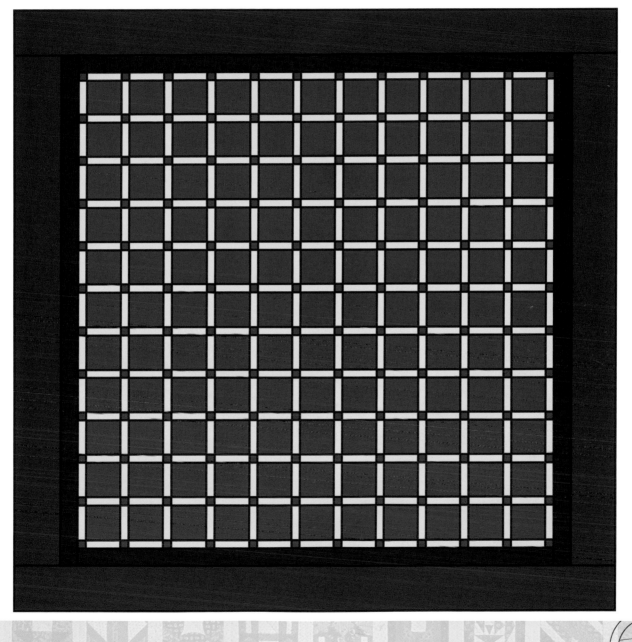

D-Cady and Katharine Herrick II

D-Cady Herrick II was born in Albany, New York on May 8, 1908. His collection of World War II letters were written home to his wife Katharine Langdon Griffin Herrick. Katharine was born on February 9, 1915 in Albany, New York. They were married on June 30, 1941 in Northeast Harbor, Maine.

D-Cady joined the United States Navy on April 17, 1942. He started his training at Quonset Point in Rhode Island, and it is there that he began to write his letters home to Katharine. He asked Katharine to save his letters as a diary of sorts, documenting his time and experiences during the war. D-Cady achieved the rank of Lieutenant Commander A USNR and was awarded a World War II Victory Medal. Two of his children, D-Cady III and Katharine, were born while he was serving in the war. A third child, Stephen, was born after the war.

D-Cady continued to serve in the United States Naval Reserves after World War II. He went on to graduate from the Albany Law School and worked as an attorney. Additionally, D-Cady was the New York State Assemblyman for the district of Albany County. He passed away on February 20, 1974. Katharine passed away on October 29, 1988.

Red Cross-Issued Sewing Kit

The Red Cross had over seven million volunteers during World War II. The aide workers presented many sewing kits to military personnel. General Eisenhower is shown here with a Red Cross worker.

D-Cady Herrick II

Katharine and
D-Cady Herrick II

D-Cady in uniform.

D-Cady sent Katharine a copy of
his Thanksgiving Day menu.

 18   D-Cady and Katharine Herrick II

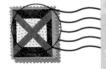

June 18, 1942

Darling,

By this time you are probably burning with curiosity to know just what has been happening here in Quonset. Most of the interesting facts are but left unmentioned, but I will try to describe the many events. On Tuesday I arrived in Providence and spent the night in the Biltmore. The bed was bumpy and the room was not attractive, but the place was crowded and I was lucky to get any room at all. Wednesday, four of us taxied out to Quonset Point, arriving here at about 9:30 a.m.

The class is composed of a group of the finest men I have ever met. They come from all over the country, any of them we would be proud to invite home to spend the night. They are grand. Up to today, we have spent most of our time doing paperwork, checking in, having our papers examined, photographed, learning our way around the barracks. The work has not begun yet, but probably will start Monday.

The subjects appear interesting and are somewhat similar to the studies I took last summer with Major Shields. Today we received inoculations. Dr. Albert Vander Veer gave me mine. He knows that I am here, but as yet I have had no chance to see him in private. We also spent about two hours drilling, just the same as our Monday nights in the armory. The officers here know their stuff, they are friendly and cooperative rather than severe. One of the first things we did was to remove all rank and wear our khakis and nameplates. We expect to get a good deal of work and very little time off.

All the student officers sleep in one compartment in double deck beds. Mine is an upper. We go to bed at 2200, 10:00 p.m. to you, and get up at 6:00 a.m. The meals are huge. This morning I had coffee, bread, butter, cereal, milk, cream, sugar, sausage and an orange. For lunch we had fish chowder, fish fried, mashed potatoes, salad, radishes and apple pie. For supper, tea, stew, potatoes, beans, peas, cake and ice cream. Anyone who complains about the meals here is crazy, they are fine, the only objection is that we get too much.

Life here is different than at home, it is much more like Lawrenceville. I miss you very much but I am proud to be able to serve in any way that I can. All my love to you, but do give some to Mother and Dad.

Devotedly,
Dick

Arrival at Quonset

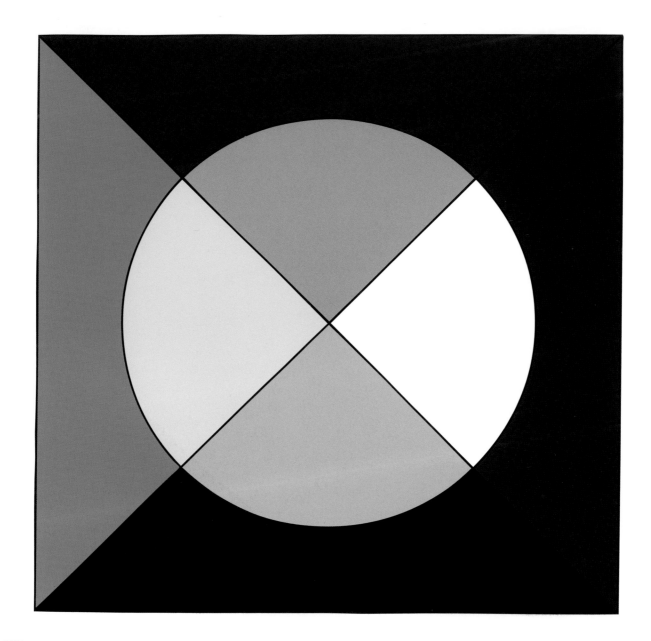

D-Cady and Katharine Herrick II

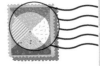

July 20, 1942

Darling,

We have just finished a week of examinations. I have heard from four of my five subjects, and while the exams were not first in the class, still they are all at least 3.4s. The other subject I have not heard from is the toughest for me. It is aviation and involved names, a complete understanding of the various mechanical operations of the parts of the engine, the wings, the tail, etc. It is quite a course, and while I am learning the subject, my mark will probably not be as good as those in the other subjects. I expect that next semester the subject will be easier. It is vastly interesting, but you know how mechanical I am.

I was invited to a cocktail party by Commander Holt the other night and discovered that Mrs. Holt was a Miss Dow (I think that is the way her name was spelled). She is related to the Kitty Lancings. You might ask Aunt Bertie if she is familiar with any of that family history. Incidentally, if you come down here again, Mrs. Holt has asked that you stay with her. Commander Holt is the third ranking officer here.

The paper punches you sent arrived and have been in constant use ever since, thank you very much. We were paid $310 today, which I can't figure out, so we had better keep a record of it and total our income at the end of the year. Our income today from the insurance department has been $1100 or $200 a month for five and half months or up to June 15. The next date is July 20, when we received $310. I am sending you a money order for $200 and keeping the balance to pay my current bills here: uniforms, laundry, government insurance, etc. I shall try to keep a record and let you know later what the total is.

The news that you send from time to time about next March is very wonderful and thrills me to no end! Dearest, I am very happy for you and also for me. This is something I have wanted for a long time. I am very proud of you and I'm confident that "our little bundle of joy" will be up to all our expectations and dreams. If Uncle Dr. feels that you should not travel, then don't plan to come down again, but I shall miss you ever more than I do now, which is terribly.

We do have a graduation of sorts, but it will be very little, quite crowded, rather formal, mostly outdoors, and will require quite a bit of walking. You and Mother had better make up your minds about coming. If you decide to come, you should arrive about the 12th and leave on the 14th late. All my love.

Your Devoted Husband,
Dick

Our Little Bundle of Joy

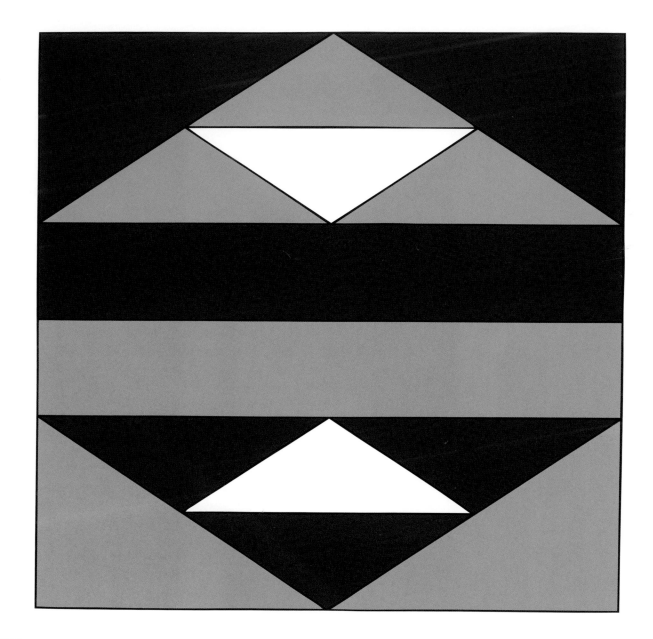

D-Cady and Katharine Herrick II

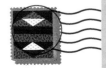

August 2, 1942

Dearest,

Your postcard has arrived. I love you very much and I am very proud that Uncle Dr. reports the condition as definite. You must have missed the letter I wrote you, it should have arrived in Slingerlands on Friday for Saturday delivery. I am sure that Mother will forward it to you, most of the information in it was repeated in my letter to your mother and father.

Van has been ordered on sea duty so his hours will be vacant in a couple of weeks. I'm trying to get it. Continuing school for two months more here puts an entirely different outlook on graduation. The ceremony itself is not too important. It will be more important to the next class because most of them will be probationary officers rather than fully commissioned officers. The really important point is that I want to be with you, and since I have to be on duty here, you probably would like to look around and find something suitable. Please let me know when you can come down because we are going to have quite a bit to do here and very little time in which to do it.

Graduation week is going to be very busy and most of the hotels etc. are already booked for August 12, 13 and 14. I shall try to make some arrangements, unless we can find a house first, for you to stay on the station. So, don't be surprised if you get a telegraph to arrive at the stated time and day. I am enclosing a graduation pass for you which is good only for the dates and gates, if you came by car as you stated. All my love, and do be careful. I miss you terribly.

Your Devoted Husband,
Dick

Graduation Ceremony

24

D-Cady and Katharine Herrick II

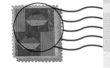

Time Certainly Drags

February 26, 1944

Dearest,

   This is just a note to let you know that I love you. It has been just over a month since we were in Albany. The time certainly drags. During the past few days we have been allowed to do a few more interesting things than attend classes. Beginning Monday, I shall teach one class in recognition. That shall be quite an experience, because the little I learned in Quonset is now out of date and the system we use is different, so I shall have at least as much to learn as the class. Also on Monday for the first time we are going to start athletics, first a course in swimming, then one in judo. You had better be very well behaved when I see you next or I shall be forced to demonstrate. Perhaps you would like that? I should right now.

   Darling, I do miss you, I'm looking forward more than I can tell you to "the day," our day. Let's both hope it will be soon. The gang I have joined is beginning to round up, they're about as nice as the one in B. H. We should have a most interesting cruise. I have been told that if my work is satisfactory that I may apply for the war college as soon as we start back. The present skipper (he shall be changed later) has appointed me, among other things, photographic officer, in hope that Art's recommendation may be carried out. It is a possibility only. All my love to you, Larry and Kitten.

                              Devotedly,
                              Dick

P.S. I woke up last night hugging the pillow and trying to dream that it was you; the substitute was no good.

D-Cady and Katharine Herrick II

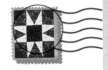

March 8, 1944

Grand Birthday Present

Dearest,

Last year was much more exciting, but this birthday is different too. Today I have the duty. Isn't that a grand birthday present? Tell Larry that I am going to eat some ice cream and cake at lunchtime just so we can have as much of a party as possible. One year can certainly go fast, can't it. It's almost no time ago at all that he arrived and yet he is almost ready to expect a sister.

You wrote me that you were going to continue my subscription to the *Rifleman*. That is fine, but have it sent to your address and then forward it to me, that way it will have a much better chance of arriving. You asked about a radio—there are no new ones out here at all so I am investigating the secondhand market. I believe that I shall be able to get one later on this month. If so, I shall let you know. One of the officers here believes he will sell his when his squadron moves, that shall be rather soon.

As the work goes along here, I seem to be acquiring new odd lots: My own liaison photographic, communications and senior member of the summary general court-martial board. That is kind of a chief judge. The Newport course is still progressing. I sent in one more section the other day, now I must wait until I hear from them.

To date I have been able to save $60, which I have mailed to you (enclosed). Please let me know if it arrives and how our account with Dr. McComber stands. Darling, I do so wish that you were out here, but it just can't be. We start our jumping around next week. I miss you terribly now and I am looking forward with dread to the next few months because your absence grows more profound every day. All my love.

Devotedly,
Dick

D-Cady and Katharine Herrick II

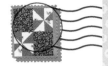

May 3, 1944

Different Squadrons

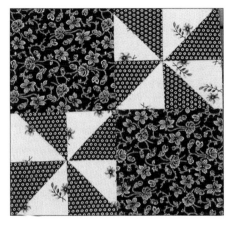

Dearest,

At long last, for some of us the fog has lifted. Our group is going to be broken up completely and sent to other squadrons. The reason, I believe, is that the Navy is expected to stick to the sea and not to the shore. Tomorrow we return once more to Alameda for a few days, probably the balance of the week. Then we expect to receive further orders taking us to different squadrons, where we do not know. My address until you hear further is either the one you have been using or CASU 6. If I don't go completely nuts, I shall be able to write clearer information within a few days.

We have moved so often out here that I am learning to pack almost as well as you do. My next object shall be to cut down the number of items I carry. Now I have my trunk, a big suitcase, the blue handbag you, Larry and Mother gave me, my ACI kits and two cruise boxes. I look like a circus. I have a hunch that I am going to Seattle and should arrive there about a week from Sunday, but this is just a guess. If I do, I shall write you and use the new address on the envelope.

Since I sent the telegram, I have been here two nights including tonight. I have been to San Diego, Los Angeles, San Francisco, Mara Island, Oakland, Alameda, all by air and all useless trips except that the authorities are trying to keep most of us together. This is going to be some good, but we are still going to learn to use new types of planes. The way things are going out here, it will take six months for any crowd to be as chummy as V 531 was. We really have been exceptionally lucky.

Darling, I miss you terribly, but I am very glad that we were not trying to keep a home out here. With the moves it just could not have been done. How is the Junior League work coming? Your plans sound interesting, you should look up our friends. Just remember that they are bound to look at the war differently than we do. All my love.

Devotedly,
Dick

D-Cady and Katharine Herrick II

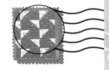

June 12, 1944

Package of Sand

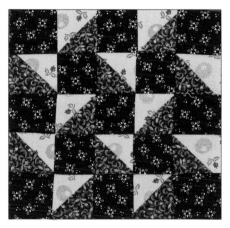

Dearest,

No letters from you and almost two weeks have gone by since the last one arrived! You were planning to leave for Ellsworth on the fifth, so I am taking a chance that you have arrived there and am addressing this as such. Did you have a good trip? I rather expect that Dickie might be a handful for you now, particularly on an all-day train ride. Did he prove so? How did you find the Bowers and what is the news of the old gang?

There is a very good possibility that the reason no mail has arrived is because the San Francisco post office has not kept close track of our changes of address. Friday, this week, we say goodbye to the desert and go back to the coast for some carrier landing practice.

You would be quite surprised if you could see me now. The sun has tanned me much darker than my khaki uniform, to a point where I rather resemble a piece of leather. Since we arrived here I have worn out three pairs of shoes just walking in the sand and have boiled off weight until I dropped down to 180 and my uniforms hang on me. If I never see a desert again, it will be too soon.

There is a great similarity between this jumping off spot and Trenton in January in a blizzard; both have about the same conveniences and both are miles from anywhere. In spite of a rather indefinite promise to give us long weekends, more have been taken because there is no way to get to town, seven miles off, that can correspond with our liberty. Some few of the enlisted men tried it the first weekend, but none have since. We just sleep aboard and hope for this Friday. It will be wonderful to take a bath in clean water, to eat food without sand and to see new faces. I have enclosed a little of the sand to let you see what it is like. All my love.

Devotedly,
Dick

D-Cady and Katharine Herrick II

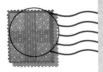

October 9, 1944

Red Cross

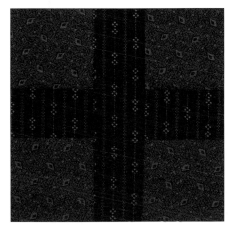

Darling,

The Red Cross came through with the most wonderful news. Kitten has finally arrived and you are fine! Congratulations and best of luck to you both, as well as my love. I have been so thrilled that I have been of no use to the Navy or to myself since. I have shown everyone, even strangers, the message I received. The squadron has all smoked cigars.

Now we must return to the grind, but when can I have a snapshot? The news has thrilled me more than I can say. I did so much want Kitten to be a Kitten and not Tom. Having two girls in the family may be a handful, but I am looking forward to the prospect. It almost seems as if the fortune teller was right.

You should have had as easy a time with Kitten as you did with Larry. I trust you did, but I am very sorry that I was not on hand to at least worry for and with you. It didn't seem to be necessary last time, but being there did make me feel somehow as if I belonged, too. Be sure you show Kitten my picture—I am sending you one—and introduce her to Daddy so that she will not be scared by the strange man who's going to come live with Mom and her someday soon I hope. If Larry is as proud of his sister as I am of my daughter, you will have very little trouble with either of the kids.

You wrote that you were surprised we were back again, we hardly got out. Our training was changed so we had to learn new tricks, how to work with the Army and the Marines in amphibious work. It seems now that I may be here long enough to vote but not to eat turkey.

I bought a small present for Kitten and for you yesterday. Kitten's will be of no use to her at all for a while, but it should seem right at the time. It's a Democratic donkey with lovely eyelashes. Possibly she can use it as a pin on her carriage, but Mother can wear it if she wishes.

Loads of Love,
Dick

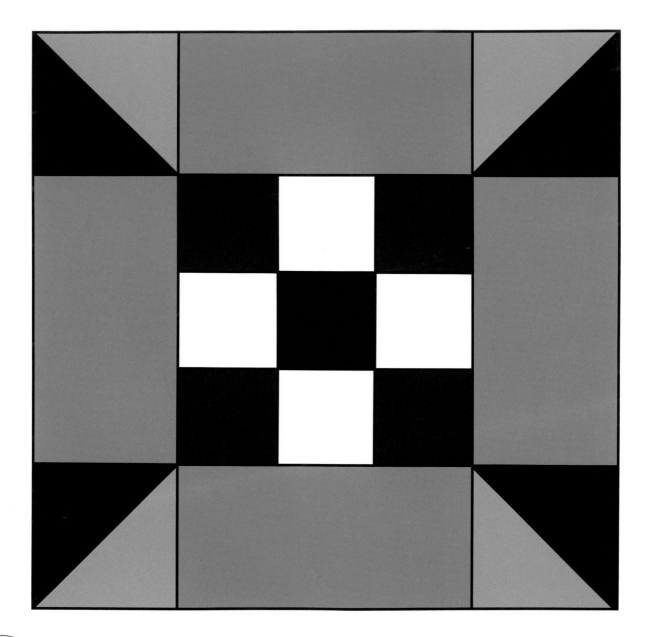

34

D-Cady and Katharine Herrick II

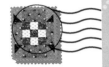

October 23, 1944

Christmas Package

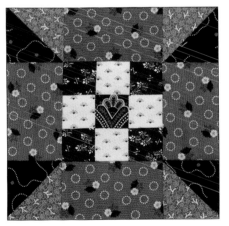

Kay Darling,

Do I ever feel like a heel! Saturday I wrote to you stating I had had no mail. This morning a Christmas package arrived plus a note from my mother and a letter from Dad. Please thank them both and give them my love. Some time ago you told me that you were sending me a Christmas package of small items etc., so I opened the box and removed the eats. They were grand and I am very fond of figs. The balance I shall keep and place under the Christmas tree on the ship, and that way I shall be sure that Santa Claus will arrive even at sea. Have you any idea what you, Larry and Kitten would like Santa to bring this year? If I get no suggestions I shall send the kids some more bonds, but I should like to send you something you would like.

The paymaster out here has been very tough so far as seapay is concerned. He says AVS officers (in the future will be A or AD rather than AVS. The A stands for air and the D stands for deck) can only draw seapay if their cruises last over half a month. Therefore mine has been "spotty," but I have unearthed an old regulation that may entitle me to seapay for several back months that should pay for all our Christmas presents and some of our bills.

Just how do we stand now — I am hoping that my promotion will come through by Christmas, if so you'll get $50 more per month and I shall pay up the balance of the bills. Loads of love.

Devotedly,
Dick

D-Cady and Katharine Herrick II

October 29, 1944

Our Squadron Planes

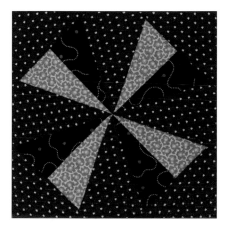

Kay Darling,

Tomorrow we move north to wait for our ship. The expectation is exciting! What will it be like? What shall we do? Where should we go? Ours should be one of the most interesting cruises of the war. It seems that we must be the real "right cross" that follows MacArthur's "left jab" to the Philippines. To say that we are hyped up is no way to express our feelings. We are nervous, jumpy, proud and scared all at the same time. Our date of leaving is most uncertain; it may be days or weeks, depending mostly on where we can find our ship and whether she needs any repairs.

Dearest, I am looking forward very much to Saturday when I shall telephone you. I am planning to place the call at about 1900 here, so you should get it in the neighborhood of 2200. I shall try to call you again after that on Thanksgiving Day, if we are here, but also when we are about to shove off. I shall not say anything about it so you will just have to guess.

What do you think of the pictures I sent you? If you don't like them, I shall have a professional one done, but the fellows here said that they thought they were good. The plane, an F6F-5 or Grumman Hellcat, is the type we are using. The one in the picture is one of our squadron planes.

Please kiss Kitten for me and tell Dickie to remember our talk. Loads of love to you, Dearest.

Devotedly,
Your Husband, Dick

D-Cady and Katharine Herrick II

June 14, 1945

Dearest,

By the time you receive this you may well be in Ellsworth. It would not surprise me in the least if this letter was to take about three to four weeks to arrive in Slingerlands. However, I shall have done my best and shall leave the rest up to Uncle Sam.

The last letter you wrote to me hinted that if we were apt to be here for any time that you would like to come out. We shall be here for a little while longer, but most of that time is going to be spent in the desert or at sea again. The dates are hectic, really dear, you would be very wise to forget the idea for the present and to look forward to next year about this time.

Life here is much the same as ever, the confounded alarms go off all day long. The newest wrinkle is the fact that they are breaking in a new bugler who is as wrong in his notes as I am in my spelling. My cabin is very nice this time. It's one designed for a lieutenant commander, but they have a third bunk in it. This consists of an iron hammock suspended from the overhead. Since I was the first on board, I have taken the lower bunk. Lieutenant Commander McBreyer has the upper bunk, and some dog's face observer sleeps in the clouds. I trust that he does not get seasick and he does not wake in his sleep, it is over six feet from the deck. I am afraid that the Army is going to have a peculiar idea of the Navy when we put him ashore again. However, I am sure that he shall see a few things that are most uncommon in the Army Air Corps.

You might try to teach Larry the difference between a boat and a ship (if he can say it safely). All my love.

Devotedly,
Your Husband, Dick

My Cabin

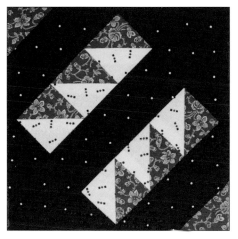

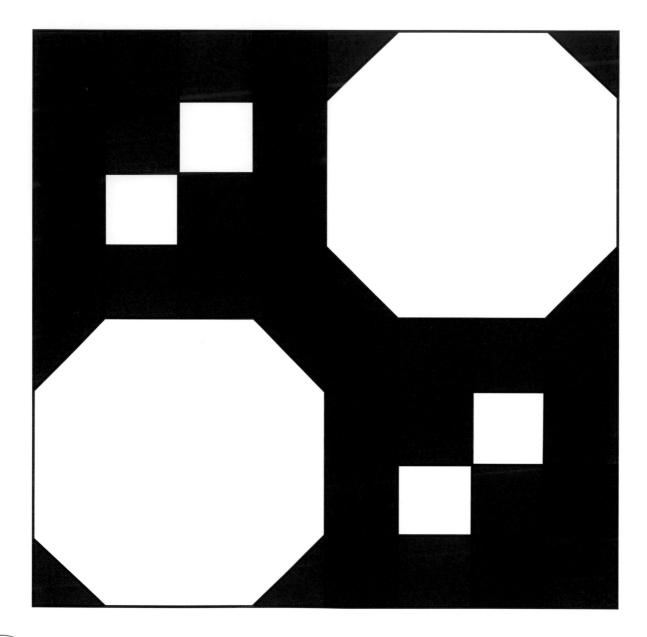

40

D-Cady and Katharine Herrick II

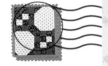

June 24, 1945

Darling,

There is very little to tell you just now. Work goes on very much as usual. For my part, work on this trip is pretty much just sitting and waiting. But even that can become tiresome. We get up about 5:00, have breakfast, then wait sometimes until 7:30, and often until 10:00, before the first flight gets off. I have a few very important (just now I hope) jobs to do before take off and on arrival. The balance of the time I must be "on top" in the ready room. That kind of progress gives me several hours of time off, most of it in a madhouse when the game is sitting around, and later at very broken intervals throughout the day.

None of it is long enough to accomplish anything in a line of uninterrupted work, and yet all together too long and too often. It is much as if you were to spend all day in the living room, with little Larry and Kitten in the next room playing. The overall picture gives you a very nice day of loafing, the details break it up.

Today I am sure that with only reasonable luck, I shall be back in time to keep our date. This year, the anniversary letter is not going to arrive on time, but before. It shall be in Maine waiting for you. A letter like that is much too intimate for me to have censored. It is something between you and me that cannot be erased by an outside world. How can they know? All my love.

> *Your Devoted Husband,*
> *Dick*

On Top in the Ready Room

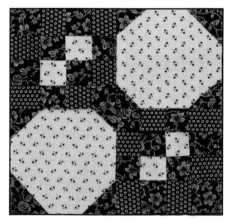

42

D-Cady and Katharine Herrick II

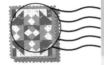

July 31, 1945

Navy Future

Dearest,

    I am very glad to hear that the doctor feels you're getting along so nicely. For some time I have felt that something more could be done about your condition, but since Uncle Arthur advised otherwise, I have raised no opinion. It's much better to get the entire thing finished now, once and for all. Then we shall not have to worry about it in the future. Now is the time to do this because we have a steady income; later on we may not be so fortunate. I rather imagine that for a couple of years after the war that the sledding is going to be tough again. We are used to that and so have no worries about it, but if we can cut out any expenses now, I believe that we will be thankful later.

    All of that reminds me, have you received our back bonds? If not, please let me know so that I can check through the problem once more. The rest you're getting should be good for you; of course, doing nothing is more trying than working at a hard job. You should learn to be patient.

    You asked about my Navy future. There is no indication so far that the Navy wants to keep any officers on as transfers to USN who are over 27. Even you, darling, are older than that now. When and if I learn of anything like that, I shall let you know. At present, the number being allowed to transfer is very small. There has been an announcement that some change is being contemplated, but to date no facts have been disclosed. The only scuttlebutt is that the authorities believe that the Navy shall be very slow in letting out any officers who are qualified for combat. The ones being let out are over age and physically limited to shore duties in this country.

    All my love to you. I miss you very, very much. By the time this arrives you should be home, and I hope completely cured at the same time. I believe I shall be on a fishing trip for a short month.

Your Devoted Husband,
Dick

D-Cady and Katharine Herrick II

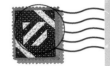

Extended Fishing Trip

August 6, 1945

Dearest Darling,

Once more we are rolling about on another extended fishing trip. From the way the news sounds, it seems quite likely that this is going to be our last wartime excursion, although it is possible that I am too optimistic. Whether it is or not is going to make very little difference to us because we believe that we shall at least be sent out to patrol duties. It is very probable that we shall be placed on some island, even Japan, to do some sentry duty. If that proves to be the case, I rather imagine that we shall be out for at least one year.

Within the next few days, I am certain that the war is going to take a surprising turn for the best. A turn that should shorten its duration by many months. This letter is not advance dope because it is not going to be mailed for at least two weeks and by then the news will be public.

The only difference that I can foresee is that we may be sent out sooner. So don't be too surprised at anything you hear or read, and don't get any false hopes either.

I love you devotedly, Darling, and miss you much more than I can ever tell you.

All My Love,
Dick

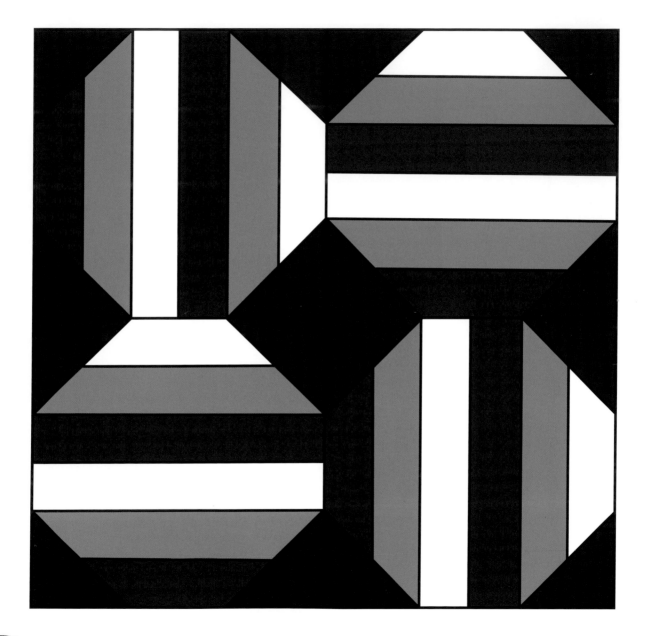

46

D-Cady and Katharine Herrick II

Free Mail

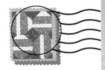

August 23, 1945

Dearest Darling,

The last letter I wrote to you I sent "free." Both of these letters are going to be mailed at the same time, so please check the arrival dates and let me know. We have found out that in many instances, the "free" mail arrives much quicker than "airmail." I do not believe that such shall be the case here with us, but it should be interesting to find out.

So far there is no news at all. We have been told that all fully trained air groups (we are one) are going to go out intact with no notice being paid to the number of points possessed by anyone. If that proves to be true, there goes my guess that our ship is going to cover the Navy's occupation of Japan.

I shall be very happy to take part in that kind of task. The work should be interesting, exciting and practical. I rather dislike the idea, however, of being bored on a small Pacific island for several months. The ship has had no news for sure for a long time now, and we are looking forward to finding bushels of letters when we get back early in September. All my love.

Devotedly,
Your Husband, Dick

48   D-Cady and Katharine Herrick II

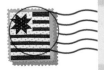

August 28, 1945

One-Week Stay

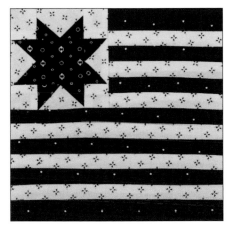

Dearest,

One of the boys aboard has just told me that Sherman Murphy is stationed in San Diego. If I can find out where he is located, I shall call him up and try to get the latest news. Julianne Hills is also located here. I saw him the day before we sailed this time. He is a captain in the Army, and at present, is teaching tactics to the Air Force training for amphibious work. I'd rather guess that he shall be out of a job before long. He looks good, just the same as ever. We had a lot of fun wondering just how Newt is making out under the point system. Both of us wish him the best of luck, and a long career in which to develop his interest in military service.

Our plan here involves about a one-week stay in the States before shipping out. This, of course, begins after the present cruise returns home. The one question involved is the exact time the ship shall be required to spend in the yards. My own guess is that we shall leave sometime about the end of September or the beginning of October. All my love to you.

Devotedly,
Your Husband, Dick

D-Cady and Katharine Herrick II

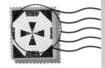

A Long Collection of Letters

September 4, 1945

Dearest Darling,

It won't be long now, probably early next week, when I hope to spend at least one full night arranging by date and then reading a long collection of letters from you. Today there is no word about any changes that might affect us. I believe that I am to go on a patrol mission to the Orient, starting probably early next month and lasting from eight months to a year. So far this is not definite, but unless something quite drastic happens which might delete all ACI from the Navy, I have no doubt but that I shall go along with the squadron. It is very probable that when we get into port, there will be some definite word. Some decision should have been made. As soon as I know, I shall let you know, but I don't expect any change. All my love to you and the kids.

Devotedly,
Dick

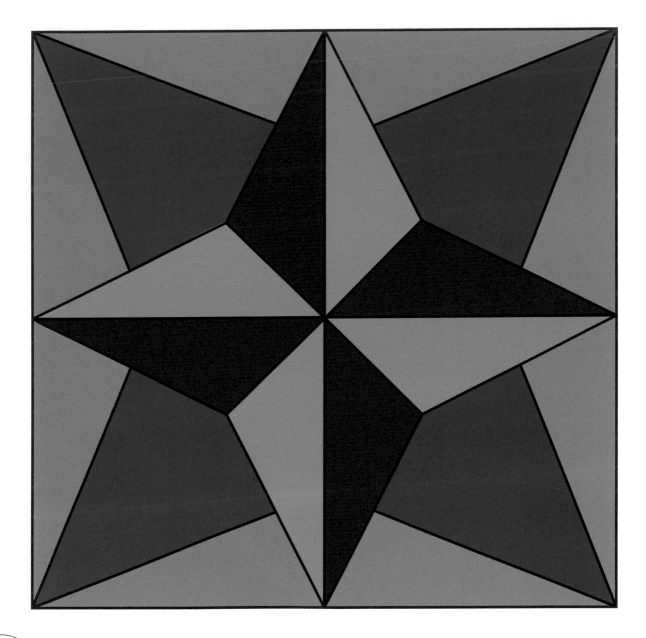

D-Cady and Katharine Herrick II

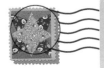

Two White Uniforms

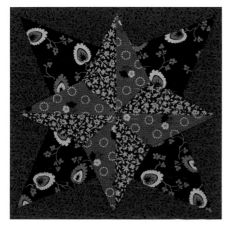

September 7, 1945

Dearest,

Within a very few days we should be back on land, probably this weekend. We did put in for Labor Day, but stood out at 0700 the following morning. I visited Sherman Murphy and Caroline. They are fine and asked to be remembered to you and Larry and your family. My love to them all, too. I bought two white uniforms from Sherman. His ship is to be commissioned soon and he hopes to be returned to Albany by Christmas.

I wrote to Mother and asked her to send me two more whites plus cap cover and shoes. They are not necessary but convenient. The Navy is going back to peacetime standards. Like Quonset all over again—we even have to take courses such as navigation, communication, etc.

You have my permission to feel sorry for me for the next several months. We are planning to do nothing but play war in training for the next one, and play it with a gang of reserves who are trained for this one and want nothing more than to get out. Won't we have a jolly time? Should you happen to drive through Brunswick, go to the college and ask for the Elsingers. Some of them, at least, should be back there about now. All my love.

Your Devoted Husband,
Dick

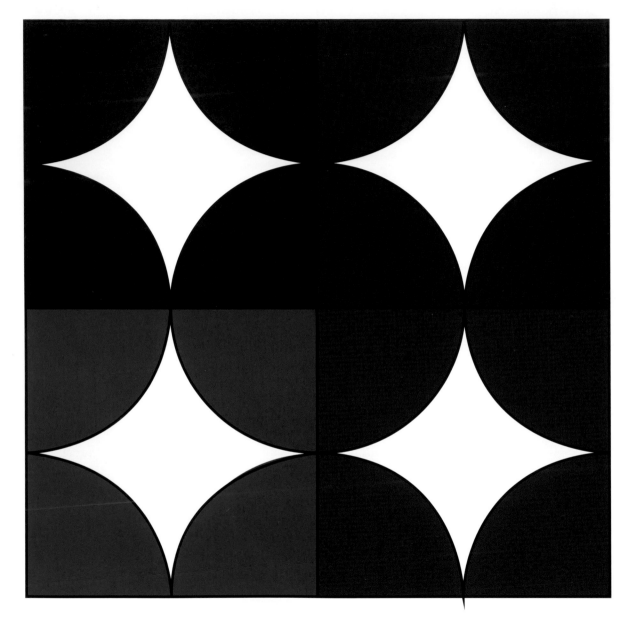

D-Cady and Katharine Herrick II

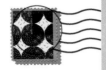

September 12, 1945

Highest Temperature 140°

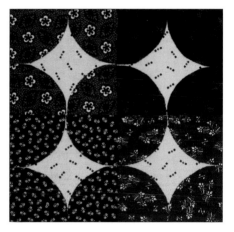

Darling,

Once more we are back ashore, and once again out in the desert. We landed Saturday, and Sunday we flew out here. The weather has not changed a bit since last time. The lowest daytime temperature has been 114° and the highest 140°. At night we do get a breeze, and at about 0430 it cools off enough to require at least a sheet. Some of the crowd uses blankets. The temperature is about 75°.

There was a grand collection of letters from you covering most of last month and part of this. I'm very glad that you have, on the whole, been having a good time in Maine. I'm happy that your trip to the hospital has proved successful. Possibly this will be the last time such work will be necessary. I hope so, you certainly deserve better luck in the future.

Today, a letter arrived from you taking my head completely off at the neck. There was no reason in my mind, I guess when I wrote it. Of course you are capable of knowing not to stay after Bill comes home. I'm sorry you believe that I thought you are stupid. Turnabout, however it is still fair play. In at least three of my last letters (again in this) I have told you there is no news out here yet about what the Navy is going to do with us. Newspapers say contrary. "Nobody knows nothing."

I still believe I'm going on one cruise, but even that is not definite. There is no reason for me to believe the Navy wants me or any ACI to turn USN. We have not been invited, so when I get out, I shall have to look for a job somewhere. As soon as I know any facts I shall let you know. There is no point in worrying about anything until we know some facts. All my love.

Devotedly,
Dick

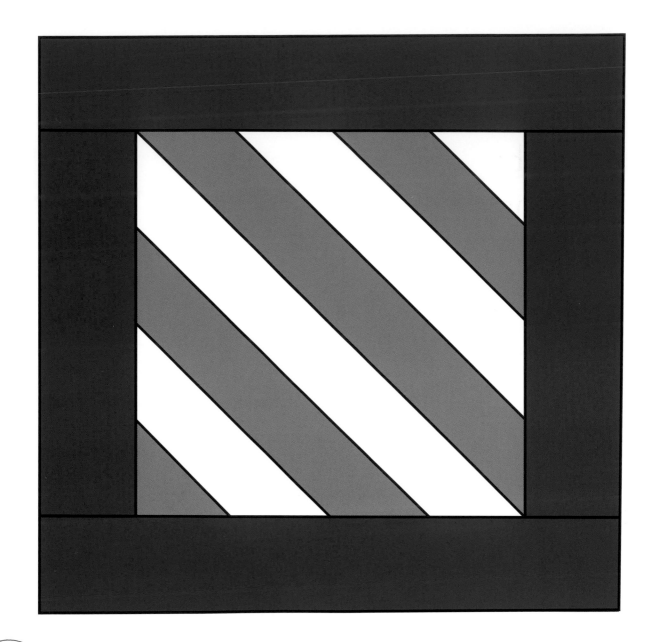

D-Cady and Katharine Herrick II

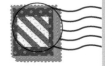

October 12, 1945

Air Combat Intelligence Officer

Darling,

Things here are in complete chaos, nobody seems to have any idea about what is going on. My case is typical. One week ago Wednesday the scuttlebutt reported that all ground officers were going to be yanked out. That afternoon we received a letter from the boss here stating that our group was an exception to the rule and that we were going to be kept with the group. The next day an order came from Washington directing all ground officers be yanked and held for further duties. On Monday, I was elected, subject to approval, to be sent to Japan to operate merchant shipping there. On Tuesday, I got word I was to be shipped to New York City for duty and probably to become a civilian. Thursday, orders taking us out of air group 38 and placing us in CASU 5 arrived and were delivered this morning. We are to be held here until someone decides what is to become of us.

In the meantime, our former ship, the USS Bairoko, demanded that Commander Fleet Air, West Coast, supply her with several essential officers including one ACI and my name was suggested. The captain of the ship and the captain in charge of personnel here have telegraphed Washington to have me given dispatch orders to the ship as Air Combat Intelligence Officer and Officer in charge of Combat Intelligence, using radar etc., practically running the ship. During this time, one of three things may happen: 1. New York City and out; 2. Japan with merchant shipping; 3. USS Bairoko. It is a free guess as to which shall come through, although, I rather believe the third one will. If so, I shall be pleasant. The job is important, and the trip would be very interesting, too. To Hawaii, Manila, Shanghai, Tokyo, and I already know all the gang aboard. All I do in the meantime is sit around and fuss, pack and repack, make telephone calls, and run around to see if any orders have arrived. All my love.

Your Fidgety Husband,
Dick

58

D-Cady and Katharine Herrick II

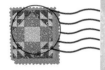

October 16, 1945

Five Letters

Darling,

Today a letter from you arrived including a rather off-color poem (thanks), and scolding me (slightly) for not writing to you often enough in the last few weeks. By my calendar—I am ahead of schedule—but, actually, since we last left the desert just before Kitten's birthday, you have been sent, not counting this, five letters. One, I believe, went to Maine and four to Albany. That is almost one letter every four days, plus two telephone calls: One when you were out and one when you were home. In return, I have received one letter stating you are leaving for Albany and that you expected to arrive the day before you did, and two since then were written on the way, so consider yourself scolded, too!

I hope your head is all healed by now. I can't answer your questions a lot, because I don't know where I'm going to be. I may be at sea, in Japan or home. Where is anybody's guess. I'll let you know by phone just as soon as I know. About going USN, I am still well above the age limit, so that is out of the question.

I do love you, Dearest. Right now, not having orders for 16 days is getting very much on my nerves and I am rather fidgety. All my love.

Devotedly,
Dick

P.S. This state of affairs should end any day now but may last to the end of October. By then I should be sure. Keep your fingers crossed.

Everett Allen and Mary Elizabeth Tucker

Everett Allen Tucker was born on January 26, 1917 in Ottawa, Kansas. One night, when accompanying a friend to a roller skating rink, Everett met Mary Elizabeth Fraker, then a junior in high school. Smitten with the young lady, he returned the following night to see her again. On October 1, 1939 the two were married in Garnett, Kansas. The couple lived here all their lives, raising their three sons, Thomas, John and Christopher.

Everett worked for the Fraker clothing company for 35 years. During World War II, he reported for duty at the US Naval training stations in Great Lakes, Illinois and then later served aboard the USS *Ajax*. He wrote his letters home to Mary, describing his training, travel, and his experiences aboard the USS *Ajax*. Everett worked in the optical shop, fixing all kinds of machinery such as clocks, watches, barometers, range finders and binoculars. He also made special jewelry for his wife in the shop.

Mary worked for the phone company until she became pregnant with her first son and decided to stay home to raise a family. After her sons were grown, Mary continued to work as a gal Friday at different offices, doing secretarial work for a deed office and a savings and loan.

Everett passed away on March 3, 1989 at the age of 72. His wife, Mary, is still living and has been a lifelong quilter.

U.S. Navy-Issued Sewing Kit

Everett Allen Tucker

Everett and Mary on their wedding day.

Mary Elizabeth Tucker

HEY! Where's That Letter You Owe Me?

I KNOW YOU'RE PUTTING ALL YOUR DOUGH

IN BONDS FOR OUR DEFENSE—

BUT AFTER ALL A POSTAGE STAMP

STILL ONLY COSTS 3¢!

THIS IS THE LATEST ARMY GAG

Everett enjoyed writing Mary letters on
postcards he collected along his journey.

Everett Allen and Mary Elizabeth Tucker

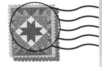

April 3, 1945

Exams at Great Lakes

My Darling Wife and Son,

Well Babe, this is one time I didn't have a reservation and am on a Pullman, so you'll have to excuse my writing as you can plainly see. I'll give you a brief description of what has happened since I called you yesterday. We got up at 4:30 in the morning, went to eat at 6:00, boarded the bus for Kansas City at 8:30, and went through preliminaries till 12:00. We went to eat, poor eats too, then took radon test till 2:30, don't know if I passed. I hope so because we get 10 months training and first seaman's rating. It's not half as bad as people say, had from three to six liberties in Kansas City. Me and my buddy from Lawrence ate (on our own money). We were going to go to a show but didn't have time. We went to the Union Station and left at 7:30 p.m. It's 9:00 now and raining like the devil. This is really a slow train. (Must have got it from Arkansas.)

We take more exams at Great Lakes tomorrow, physical and stuff. How is my boy, does he miss his daddy? His daddy misses him and you too. I love you, Babe.

Oh yes, about forgot, at Kansas City, they asked for five volunteers for Marines. Didn't get them so they picked some. Setter, the boy from home, was chosen, he was pretty blue about it. I don't blame him. My buddy's name is Montgomery, a Notre Dame man, 18 years old. He is a radar man, kind of young but a swell fellow.

Probably won't have time to write tomorrow, I hear. Well, I guess I better sign off and get some shut-eye, got a hard day ahead they say. Will write as soon as possible. Kiss Tommy for me and kiss you for me.

Lots of love,
Tuck

P.S. I may get back in the practice of writing letters yet.
XXXXXXXOOOOOOO. I love you.

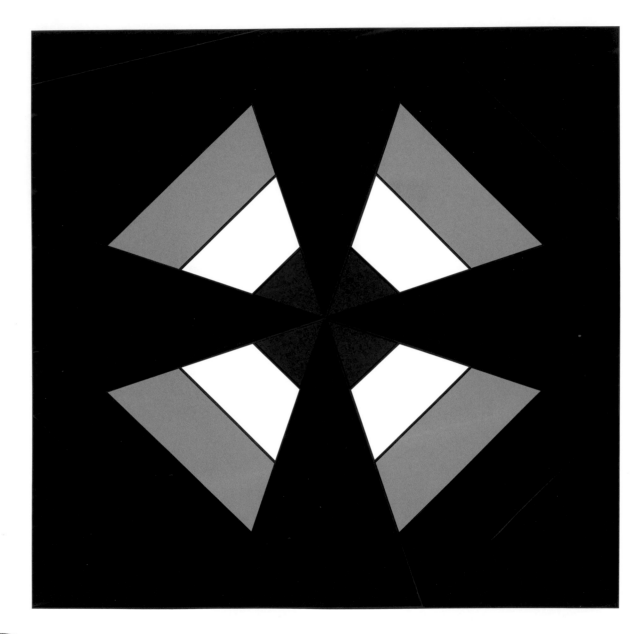

Everett Allen and Mary Elizabeth Tucker

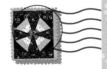

Company Commander Took Inspection

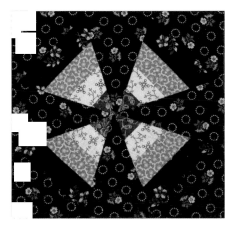

April 8, 1945

My Darling and Son,

Well, Darling, here it is Sunday, our day off. Went to church this morning. Oh yes, I guess I better tell you I slept with a bag last night, all night, a sea bag. That's what you put your clothes in. The reason was that the ends of the drawstring at the top weren't tucked in after it was tied to the jackstay. The company commander took inspection last night after the lights were out and said by God, if I can't tie it up right, sleep with it, so I did all night.

I am captain of the bulletin board and put up all notices and print all signs for it. It's 20 feet long and about six feet wide. I think I'll knock off for now and phone you collect. No money, they won't cash these checks up here, got to go to camp to do it. Couldn't get through so I'll write some more.

Everyone in the other companies around here says we have the toughest CO in the whole Great Lakes division and brother, I believe it. Have you written me yet? How is Tommy? Have you gotten him a sand pile built yet? Is Dad going to get him a dog? Does he miss his daddy? I'd sure like to see him. Is he talking much more than he did? Well, I guess I'd better go. Got to do a little cleaning up.

Oh yes, we have a radio in our barracks now, the company commander brought his over for us to use. Must close now.

With all my love for you and Tommy,
Tuck

P.S. Here's a card, scratch the last paragraph.
XXXXXXOOOOOO

Everett Allen and Mary Elizabeth Tucker

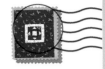

April 11, 1945

Stand
Guard

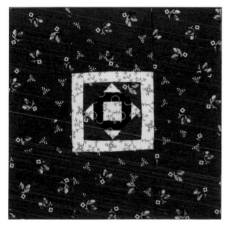

My Darling Wife and Son,

Well I guess your mail is finally catching up. I got two today and one from Mom. You don't need to send me anything because I can get things so much cheaper up here, but you might send me some cookies of some kind.

As I said before, I don't have much time to write because of the washing and cleaning up after we knock off drilling and other things. I'm sorry I only have time for a few lines a night, but I'll have more time when I get out of here, which I hope is soon. I wish my letters would reach you quicker.

You asked if we got all of our clothes. Yes, one pair of work shoes, one pair of dress shoes, tennis shoes, rubbers, two blue pants, three blue jumpers, three white pants, three white jumpers, six pairs of underwear (summer), two pairs of winter, one dozen hankies, six pairs of socks, as well as four towels, one mattress, two bed slips, one pillow, two blankets, one shaving set, one ditty bag, and one sea bag. I know this isn't all, but brother, that's enough to pack.

Darling, I love you honest and truly, lots and lots. Please believe that. I'll write you every chance I get, so if I miss once in a while, please don't feel so badly. We've been working pretty hard, but I guess it won't hurt me. I had to stand guard in the boiler room from 4:00 a.m. till 7:00 this morning. We have a long day tomorrow. Our chow is very good, steak about every other day. We get up at 5:30 a.m. and go to bed at 9:30 p.m.

Hope Tommy doesn't forget me before I come home. I'll be wearing whites when I come home. Maybe you can make Tommy a white suit by then. It's about time to knock off and go to bed, so guess I better close. I do love you, Darling.

Your loving Husband,
Tuck

Everett Allen and Mary Elizabeth Tucker

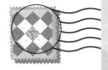

April 14, 1945

Postcard Letter

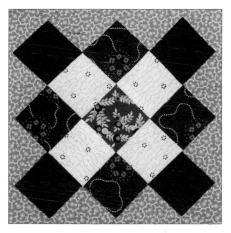

My Darling Wife and Son,

Hello Sweetheart, here I am again. I sent you some postcards last night and made it into a letter so hope some of them don't get lost. Sent you a magazine today.

We had our shots today, three of them, and I didn't walk fast enough and I got four, maybe they thought I could take it, ha. Anyway, my arm is really sore, the left one, or I would not be writing, but we had it pretty easy this afternoon. Some of the fellows passed out during inspection this morning, I think.

I just got your package, Darling, thanks a lot. I saved out about a dozen cookies for myself, really good. Boy, have I got the washing to do. Hope my arm isn't as sore tomorrow as it is today or I might not get it done. I fixed a guy's watch this afternoon, now the CO wants me to fix his. Got to get some suck in somewhere.

Got a letter from Mom today. She's doing all right, three from her since I've been here. She said she had a long one from you the other day. Just heard a guy in the lower barracks has scarlet fever or something, may get quarantined. I hope not, don't want to stay here any longer than I have to. We have a fellow in our barracks who sure reminds me of Billy Shepherd, blonde hair, only darker, about the same build and about the same type.

Darling, I sure love you, no foolin', lots, lots more than I really thought I did, honest. Gosh, I'd like to see Tommy. Golly I miss both of you. Say, by the way, don't you think I'm doing pretty good at writing you? How about sending a piece of that stuff in a separate package special delivery? I guess I'm going to have to keep the carbon copies of the letters I write you. I'm afraid I duplicate too much. Must close, Darling, and hit the sack. I love you very, very, very much.

Your Hubby,
Tuck

Everett Allen and Mary Elizabeth Tucker

Mother's Day Present

May 13, 1945

My Darling Wife,

   Just a note of excuse, cannot get your Mother's Day present till the middle of the week. Sorry. You'll probably get it about next Sunday anyway. Here's to a very loving mother and devoted wife, from me. Must close.

All my love,
Tuck

P.S. I hear we graduate the 24th and leave a week later. So go to the doctor and get prepared. Please make my excuse to your mom (our mom), and tell her that we don't have too much to choose from up here and I hope your present will do for the both of us. Kiss Tommy for me.

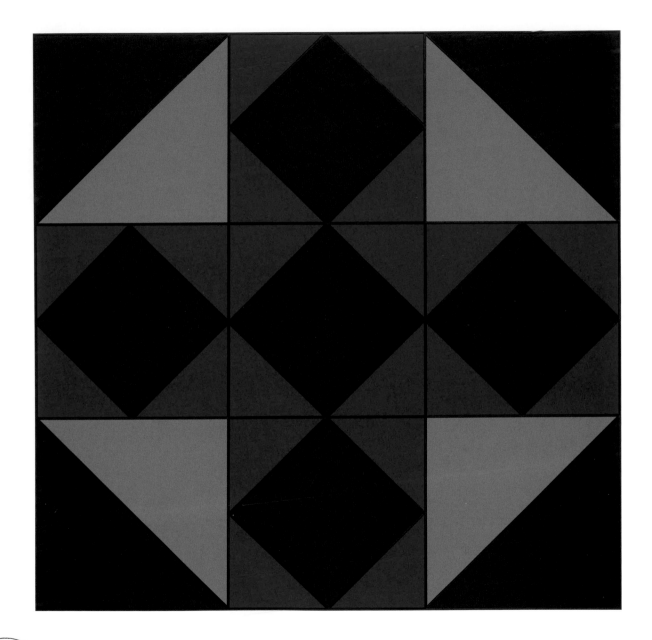

Everett Allen and Mary Elizabeth Tucker

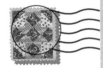

June 26, 1945

My Darling Wife and Tommy,

   Well Sweets, we're on our way, have been since 12 p.m. It's 7:00 now and we're only 75 miles out of Chicago. Council Bluffs, Iowa is our next stop. The worst part is chair cars all the way to California, so hope we have a few days to recuperate after we get there. Boy, this sure is a rough stretch of track. By the way, our car is gaslit, nothing but the best for the armed forces.
   I'm going to write to Mrs. Whitney and get Whit's address now that I know where I'm going. We have 24 cars on our train, four of them are Army from France going to the Pacific.
   You should be home by now. Hope Tommy hasn't forgotten you, give him a great big kiss for me and tell him I love him. I'm going to miss not being with you every night, Darling. I did enjoy it very, very much. Better close, Sweets, with all my love.

Your Hubby,
Tuck

PS. I'll write you again tomorrow
XXXXXXXXXXXXX

All the Way to California

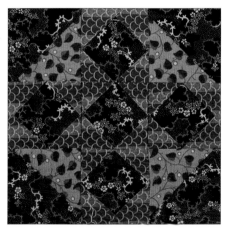

Everett Allen and Mary Elizabeth Tucker

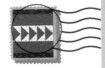

June 28, 1945

Postal Money Orders

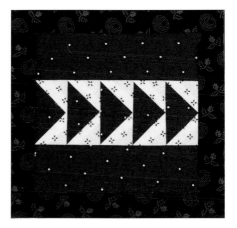

My Darling Wife,

Hello, Sweetheart. Well, here we are in Colorado. We left Denver this morning about 10:30, passed through 30 tunnels, one that was seven miles long. Saw some of the most beautiful country, practically were on a snowcapped mountain, and we've been following the Colorado River for the last three hours. We are in cliff country now. We stopped to take in coal and water and a bunch of us took a sponge bath. They wouldn't let us go swimming. Till then we all looked like a bunch of hogs, none of us has shaved since we left. I don't know any of the places' names we went through since Denver except one, Pinecrest. Maybe you can find it on a good map. There were lots of cabins there and a small stream running through the middle. We were up to an altitude of 9,671 feet this morning. I took some pictures of some of the things I saw. I hope they're good, but the train was moving so I don't know. You can have them enlarged about four times and have some pretty good scenery.

Will you send me some postal money orders? I don't know how long I'll be at the Shoemaker and I want to have a good time. If I'm there long enough, I'll have you come out. Also I need some new undershirts, to get my clothes cleaned, and a few other things. Can you send $50 and send it registered? I know it sounds like a lot, but I probably won't be here too long. Send it as soon as you get this and I should get it a couple of days after I get there.

I just looked up and we're in a desert or something, the sagebrush won't hardly grow. Another tunnel coming up. Wasn't that bad, three blocks long. Looks like they are building a new road along the river. Maybe it will be done when the war is over. Just went through Derteso, that may not be on the map either. Anyhow, I love you, Darling, and will write again tomorrow if I can find some stationery.

Lots of love,
Your Hubby

P.S. Kiss Tommy for me.

Everett Allen and Mary Elizabeth Tucker

Nothing but Sagebrush

June 29, 1945

My Darling Wife and Son,

Here I am again. We just went through a dust storm about like the ones we used to have in Kansas. We got into Salt Lake City about 9:00 this morning, and from what I saw, I didn't think it was so hot. The lake itself is really big, though. Since we left, I haven't seen such godforsaken country. I wouldn't take the whole state as a gift, nothing but sagebrush and not much of that.

There really isn't much to talk about except sand dunes and that's not very interesting. Everyone says we are going to San Pedro now instead of Shoemaker. I guess that means "an fibs" if we do. Figured I might as well tell you now as later. I'll know for sure by the time you get this letter. Coming into a town, so guess I better close and mail this. Am going to write Mom later on today. I love you very, very much, Darling.

Your loving Hubby,
Tuck

P.S. I love you. Kiss Tommy for me.
XXXXXXXOOOOOUUOOO.

Everett Allen and Mary Elizabeth Tucker

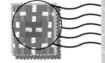

Enough Liberty

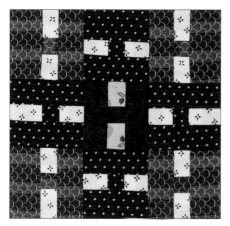

June 30, 1945

My Darling Wife,

Well, here I am, Darling, in Los Angeles. We were here for about an hour, so I called Ray and he gave me Ruth's phone number. Boy, he was really surprised to hear me. Wants me to call him if I get enough liberty to come up. Sis was surprised too, she's coming down to see me when I know where I am. I tried to call Clyde, but no one was home.

It will feel a little more like home with all the relations so near, if you call 130 miles near. Notice I said a little more, because nothing could take the place of what I've got. If you haven't sent the money yet, hold it for a while. Ruth said she would let me have some and you could send it to her. Hope they don't put us in the Fleet Marines.

I miss you, Darling, lots and lots. Guess I better close and I'll mail this. I'll write you as soon as I know anything. I love you lots and lots, Darling. Kiss Tommy for me.

Your loving Hubby,
Tuck

P.S. I have to use the old address as I don't know the new one.

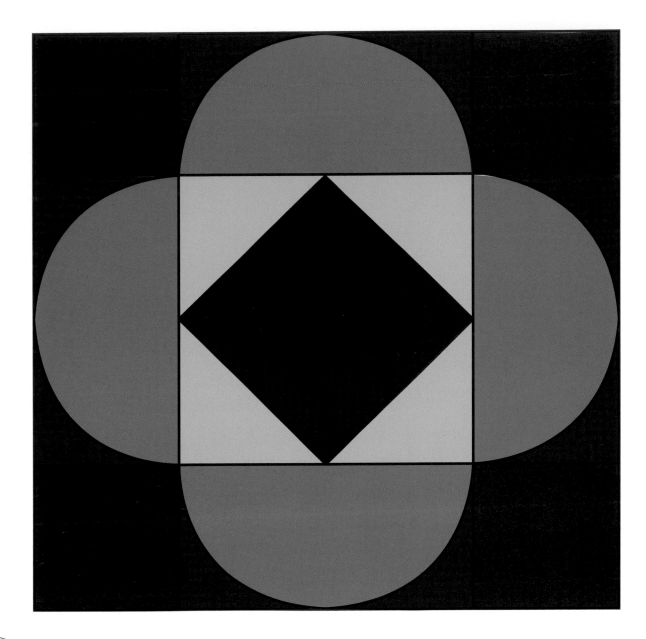

Everett Allen and Mary Elizabeth Tucker

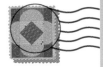

July 1, 1945

Very Nice Camp

My Darling Wife,

Hello, my Sweet. How are you today? It took us from 9:00 yesterday morning till 7:00 last night to get to this camp. It's way back in the sticks about 13 miles from Diago and four miles from Linda Vista. Some of the fellows say we will be here anywhere from two days to two weeks. This is just another distribution center like O.G.U. It's really a very nice camp, the chow is wonderful compared to the chow back at the lakes.

I'm going to try to get liberty next weekend and see Sis and some of the relations in L.A. I wish you could be there and on the other hand I might not be here by then. This camp is way up in the hills and used to be a Marine camp. This sure doesn't seem like Sunday to me. Boy, did I sleep good last night. Didn't wake up once.

Guess I'd better sign off for now and go muster. I'll write you again tomorrow, Darling. I love you very much.

Your Hubby,
Tuck

P.S. We can get a carton of cigarettes a week here. Kiss Tommy for me. Wish some letters would come through so I could hear how he was and you, too.

82

Everett Allen and Mary Elizabeth Tucker

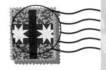

August 2, 1945

My Darling Wife and Son,

Can't say very much so please excuse. Lester seemed down in the dumps when we saw him Sunday, didn't he? Are you going to send me the top to my fountain pen? I bought a bottom off a kid for two bucks. You should have seen me about the first two days out, boy, was I sick. A lot more were the same way, so I didn't feel so bad. Give my regards to Alice when you see her next, and say hello to Sally.

I'm sorry our plans didn't turn out the last day I was there, but maybe it was best because it would have been all the harder to leave you if they had. Wish I could have seen our boy before I left. Be sure and give me all the latest about him.

We got two more shots yesterday and think we get two more in the near future, sometimes I think it's just routine. I've found out one thing, though—the only ship I want to see is the one that brings me back. Guess I wasn't born a water dog. Ha ha. Not much more room, Darling, and there isn't a thing to write about. We have been having good chow three times a day, hope it keeps up. Can you write Doyle and give him the latest? Have lots of letters waiting on me, Darling. I love you very, very much, please remember that, and kiss Tommy for me. Must sign off. All my love.

Your Hubby,
Tuck

Good Chow

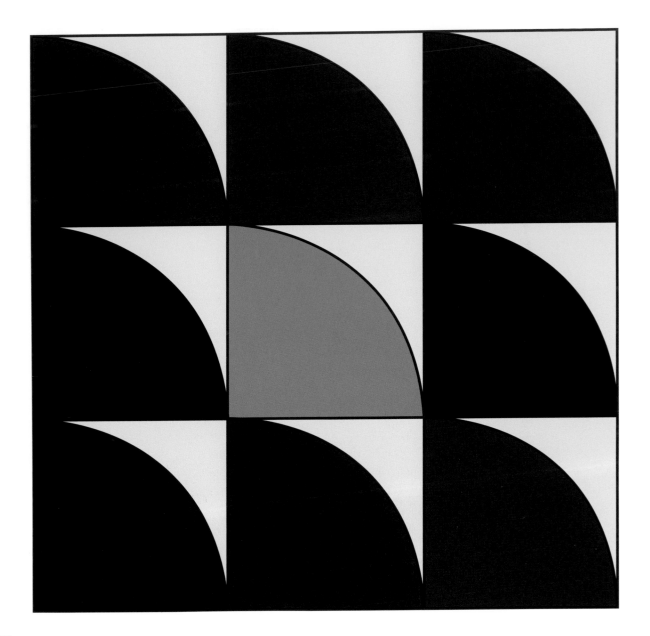

Everett Allen and Mary Elizabeth Tucker

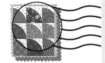

Optical Department

August 25, 1945

My Darling Wife and Son,

Hello, my Sweets, I expect you thought I had forgotten you but, my Darling, I didn't. It's just that we couldn't mail anything till we got assigned. I haven't received any mail since we left and probably not for another three weeks. Don't get me wrong, I know it isn't your fault. All of my buddies got small crafts so now I'll have to find some more. Tell my mom that Chuck Andrews' brother is aboard.

I'm sure lucky to get this ship, it one of the best in the Navy. Hot and cold water 24 hours a day, the best chow (outside of home), all you want. In fact, all the comforts of home, including the basement I have (except you).

When I go ashore, I'm going to get a set of mother of pearl to have some earrings and a ring made for you and some other stuff. I want you to send me some real bright colored sheet print material, six or seven yards, to sell the natives. I expect you think I'm nuts, but I'm really not. We haven't been paid since we left, but I'll send you some money in the near future. The chief of police aboard is trying to get me in the optical department repairing watches and things like that. Must close for now, will write soon. All my love.

Your Hubby,
Tuck

P.S. I love you.

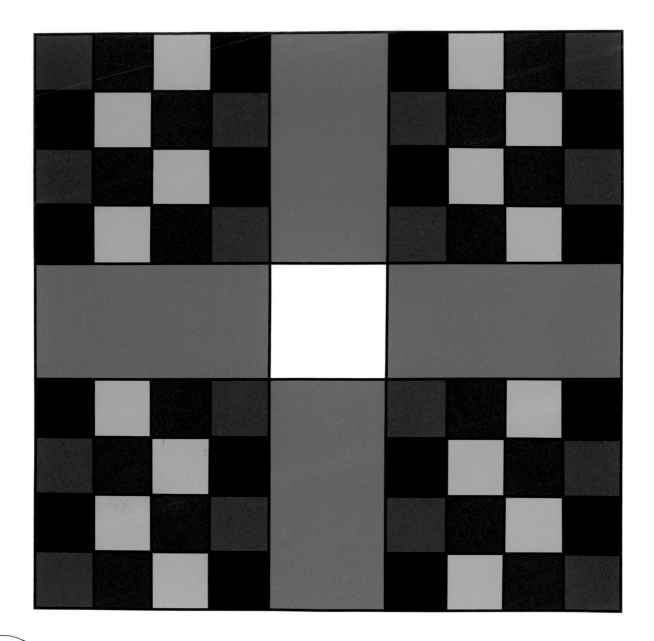

Everett Allen and Mary Elizabeth Tucker

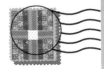

September 2, 1945

Could Not
Go Ashore

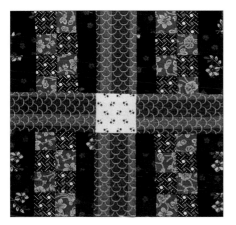

My Darling Wife and Son,

Here it is still Sunday, guess I never told you where all I have been. The first stop we made was at Eniwetok in the Marshall Islands, which has about 10 palm trees on the whole island and I think a good size wave would wash everything off it. From there we went to Ulithi in the Caroline Islands, which is a little larger. We couldn't go ashore either place, so yesterday was the first time I have had my foot on good solid ground for six weeks.

What was the last word you heard from Bud? I imagine how happy the folks were when they heard of the surrender. You, too, of course. I hope we're home by next July and kind of think we might be; of course, that's just wishful thinking.

Has Dad been squirrel hunting yet this fall? Sure would like to be there when quail season opens. This will be the second I've missed in five years, and to think they'll probably have plenty of shells this year, too. Has Harold ever painted my boat? He said he would for using it.

Well, the two letters today kind of made up for the ones I didn't write, don't they. So guess I better sign off. All of my love.

Your Hubby,
Tuck

P.S. Tell Mom I'll write her soon. Kiss Tommy for me.

Everett Allen and Mary Elizabeth Tucker

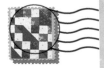

September 4, 1945

To the Sweetest Wife in the World: My Darling,

Well, what do you think of that? No more censor, so I guess I can tell you a few things you don't know. This is a fleet repair ship, Darling, just like a big factory with more machinery than you can shake a stick at. The ship is about 600 feet long with a 90 foot beam. I am in one of the best branches on the ship, in the optical shop. We fix binoculars, rangefinders, typewriters, watches, clocks, barometers and most everything. We have a small machine shop where I fix barometers at present, and since the fleet is in Japan, we don't have much work. As soon as some of the 44 point men leave, I'll get into the watch shop. The big machine shop below deck fixes everything, including big holes in ships, propellers and such. Our place is about three decks above the main deck, all air-conditioned, and I sleep up here on an army cot with two blankets at night. I've been making rings with a mother of pearl set the last few days as there's no work.

The lieutenant in charge of us is from Wichita, lives in Waco and has been in 20 years. His name is Persons. My bosses are swell and so are all the fellows that work here. The USS Ajax has been out here 22 months and is supposed to go back around the first of the year, keep your fingers crossed. When we do, we will probably go to San Francisco. I see that Kansas is going to give $300 mustering out pay, and with the government's contribution we can buy furniture. Okay?

Well, I guess that just about covers everything. In another letter I'm sending some pictures of our celebration the other night. Thousands of dollars went up in smoke, it was really pretty, skyrockets and flares. Oh my Darling, I'll be so glad to get home and be with you and Tommy. Honestly Sweets, you'll never know how much I love you and long for one of your kisses. Oh, yes I'm making you a ring, too. Haven't sent the box yet. I love you so very much, honest I do. Guess I better close now, as I have a watch to stand. Does this letter make up for some I didn't write? Hope so. All of my love.

Your Hubby,
Tuck

P.S. Kiss Tommy for me and have him give you three for me. Does he talk much yet? I love you, Darling. XXXXXXXXXXXXXXXXXXXXXXXXXXXXXXXXXXXXXX
(Couldn't do this before on account of censorship)

No More Censor

90

Everett Allen and Mary Elizabeth Tucker

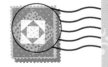

September 18, 1945

Shoving Off

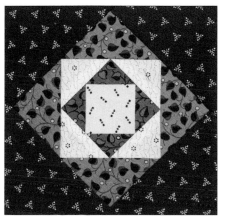

My Darling Wife and Son,

Well, it finally came. We are shoving off for Okinawa the 20th (going to have a four-hour trial run tomorrow), so by the time you get this, we'll be there. From there, no one seems to know. Anyway, we will be about 200 miles closer to home. I got out all your letters, read them all over and threw most of them away. Since I'm getting some now, I don't need the old ones.

I've got a terrific headache tonight for some reason. Anyway, when we get up there, the climate won't be so hot and sticky, should be almost like it is at home (I hope).

I suppose you're wondering what I've done aboard. I fixed three instruments! Ha ha! And the rest of the time we play cards — Rook, rummy, casino — and make trinkets for you, mostly cause it's so near like being at home with all the equipment we have. Would you like anything special? Guess I'm going to have to knock off for tonight, Darling. My head hurts so bad I can hardly see. Anyway, you know now that you won't be getting any letters for almost four or five days interval.

I love you, Darling, very, very much. Will mail my next letters as soon as possible. All of my love.

Your Hubby,
Tuck

P.S. Kiss Tommy for me, I love you both lots.
XXXXXXXXXXXXXXXXX

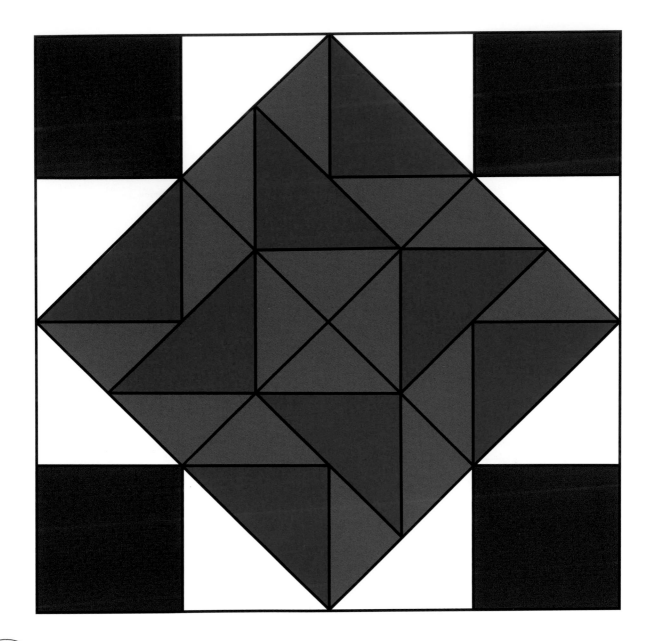

Everett Allen and Mary Elizabeth Tucker

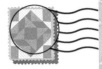

October 12, 1945

Near a Typhoon

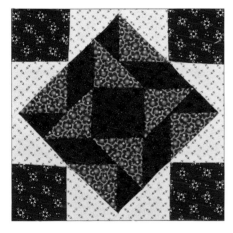

My Darling Wife and Son,

Well Darling, here we are back at Okinawa after about five days cruising around in the China Sea. Every time we go out to sea I have a watch to stand, and it seemed like this time it was every time it rained. I'll try to give you some idea what it's like to be near a typhoon (near being about 150 miles from it). The swells sometimes are higher than your head when you're standing on the main deck. That's two decks lower than the optical shop. Once in a while the bow of the ship will nosedive right into one, and the water is almost six inches deep on the deck. You are standing in the shop and the first thing you know, you are running to the other side on account of the tilting of the ship.

I'm glad we weren't here when it hit this time, as it was around 100- to 125-mile an hour winds. Lots of small craft were reefed and one or two capsized. A couple of tankers and another craft broke in half. Our convoy picked up four to five survivors and one dead about three hours out of the harbor today. The post office blew away and the hospital, along with all the round-topped huts. So, we probably won't get any mail for a while.

All 44 point men went to the beach the day before we left, so they are probably scattered to the high winds by now. I think most of the men got back into the hills, but there were about 500 dead they think. I'm sure glad I didn't have enough points to get off while we were here.

Well, guess I better close for now, Sweets. I love you very, very much. Tell Tommy hello and kiss him for me. Will write again tomorrow, so until then, all of my love.

Your Hubby,
Tuck

P.S. I love you.
S.W.A.K.

94

Everett Allen and Mary Elizabeth Tucker

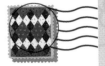

November 22, 1945

Thanksgiving Dinner

My Precious,

Well, first of all, we had Thanksgiving dinner today, and this is the menu. We had it today instead of next week because we'll have a lot of extra passengers aboard then. Anyway, here's the dope. We leave next Sunday, as I said before. The captain issued an order that all men with less than 29¾ points or a year's sea duty would be transferred off. I have only 29¼, but our division officer wanted to keep me and another fellow, so he went to bat, and as it stands now, I come with the ship. Could be that my being in the watch shop helped a little too, because soon as we get to the States, I'll be the only one in here, as the other fellow has enough points.

I asked him tonight how my chances were, and he said I don't think you got anything to worry about. We're going to take on about 800 passengers, maybe tomorrow. By the way, keep your fingers crossed till you hear my call. Anyway, I got two more packages and the American magazine. Yesterday the box of candy came, excellent, not even hardly soiled. Boy, was it good.

Did I ever tell you about the clock? It has a black and white transparent base and case and a red dial like the sample you have. It really is a sizzler. I know you like it. Haven't had much watch work this week, don't know how come. I'm all caught up, too. Guess I've told you everything there is to tell, so guess I'll sign off.

I love you very, very much, Darling. May not get to see you at Christmas, but I'll probably see you around the first of the year for about 15 days. All of my love.

Your Hubby,
Tuck

P.S. I love you. Kiss Tommy.
XXXXXXXXXOOOOOOO

Everett Allen and Mary Elizabeth Tucker

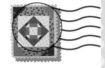

December 20, 1945

Pictures From Honolulu

My Darling Wife,

Well, Sweetheart, here we are at San Francisco, came under the Golden Gate at 1 p.m. We are moving to Hunters Point tomorrow. I had the watch as we were pulling in today, and brother, was it cold. From what I hear, transportation is really tough here. There are around 100,000 discharged men waiting on transportation. I don't think I'm going to get leave for about 20 to 30 days, so your folks better go ahead and have Christmas, and you and I will have ours when I come home. Okay?

My call cost $7.85 the other day. We must have talked quite a while. I waited almost two hours for them to get the call through. Boy, am I going to do a lot of arguing if anyone tries to sell sunny California to me. Brr, it's cold.

I've got two or three presents for you but I'm not sending them and I'm not going to tell you what they are. Curious? Ha ha. I bought about $80 worth of parts from the guy who was here and got discharged. I didn't pay for all of it because I didn't know how much money I'd make between now and when I come home. May call you again one of these days, it probably will be a Sunday so I can talk to Tommy, too.

I'm sending some pictures from Honolulu. Can't think of much more to say, Darling, except I love you very much. I am anxious to see you. All of my love.

Your Hubby,
Tuck

P.S. Kiss Tommy for me. I love you.

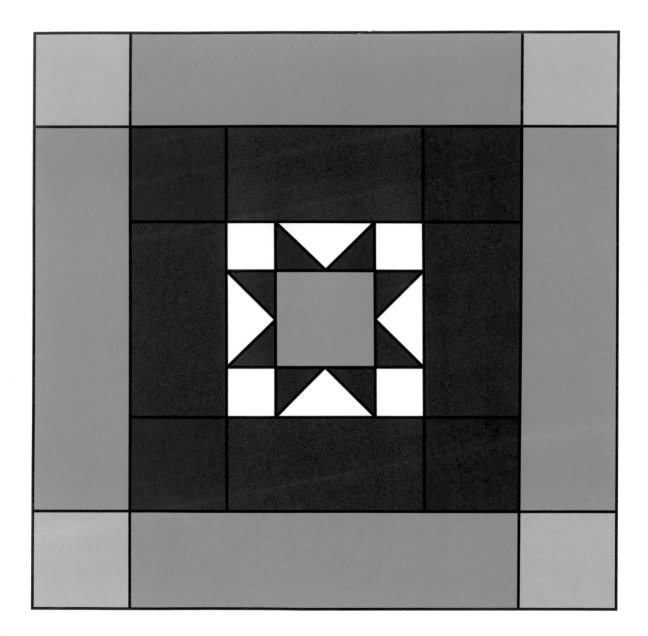

98

Everett Allen and Mary Elizabeth Tucker

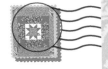

December 26, 1945

A Nice Christmas

My Darling Wife and Son,

You're probably wondering what all this is, some pictures, a couple of menus from our party. Tasted champagne for the first time and it's just like Bill's home brew except more of a wine taste. Do you think I've changed so much from when you last saw me? I only weigh 158 stripped now. I'm almost caught up with you. Ha ha.

I've got a surprise for you and you don't have to guess what because here it is: I get 21 days and traveling time of about six days. How's that? I'm just as happy as you are. Hope Tommy had a nice Christmas, even without his daddy. What all did he get?

I am sure glad to hear that Bud is on his way home. Hope we can be home the same time. You know it rained every day since we pulled in here. Did I tell you I traded the traveling clock I made for a pair of brand-new binoculars? Well, I did anyway. They're worth about $90.

Do you still love me, Darling? Or need I ask? I love you more than anything in the world. Can't think of anything else to say, so guess I better close. All of my love.

Your Hubby,
Tuck

P.S. I love you, I love you, I love you. OOOOOXXXXX

100

Everett Allen and Mary Elizabeth Tucker

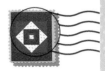

Working Pretty Hard

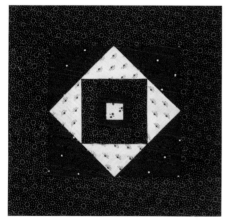

January 18, 1946

My Dearest Darling,

I'm sorry, Sweetheart, I haven't been writing as often as I should, but I've been working pretty hard, pulling strings, etc. You see, I'm making a clock similar to mine for the Lieutenant Commander. He is letting me leave at 6 a.m. Monday to catch the daylight limited to L.A., which will get me there at 6 p.m. I'll rest and catch the El Capitan on Tuesday.

If Ruth does her part, I'll call you when I get to L.A. Oh, Darling, I can hardly wait. I'm sorry I haven't written you. It's not that I haven't been thinking of you. I'll make it up when I see you. Wait and see. I should be there about Thursday, hope the ghost has come and gone by then.

Well, I guess that covers about everything except I love you very, very much. You're going to be so nice to sleep with again, and after my leave it won't be very long till I can every night. All of my love.

Your Hubby,
Tuck

P.S. I love you, I love you, I love you.
XXXXXXXXXXXXXX

Clarence and Floy Falstrom

Clarence E. Falstrom was born on August 1, 1907 in Kansas City, Kansas. It was here that he met and married his sweetheart, Floy Reiber. The two continued to live in Kansas City, where Clarence worked as a chemist, a control operator for the power company and an amateur radio operator. Floy worked as a secretary in various offices around Kansas City both during and after the war.

Clarence served in the Navy in 1923 and 1928, then later served in the National Guard until 1930. He was a corporal in the Signal Corps during World War II. He wrote Floy a couple of times a week and was always taking plenty of photographs to send home to her. His letters are written on small note cards with a variety of different pictures on them.

After the war, Clarence and Floy remained in Kansas City. Clarence passed away on August 9, 2000 at the age of 93 and Floy passed away in 1995.

U.S. Army-Issued Sewing Kit

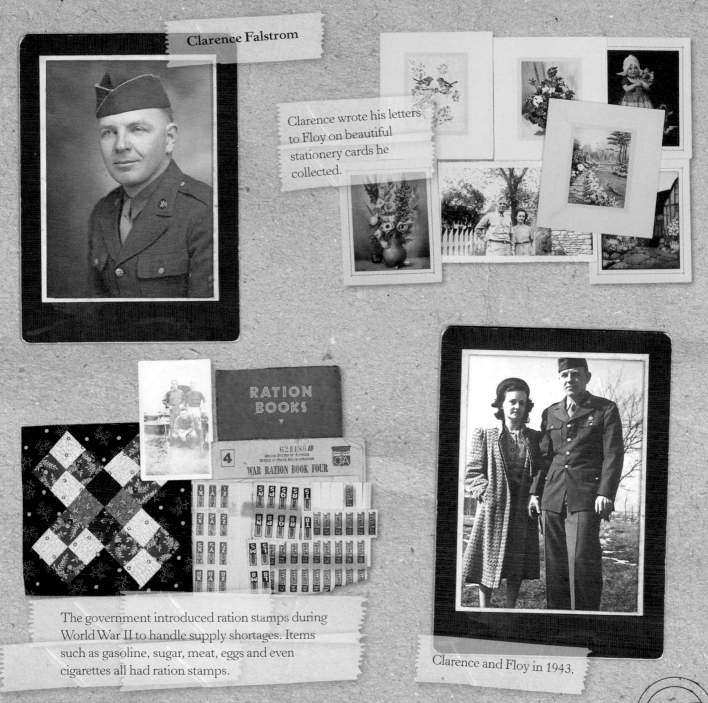

Clarence Falstrom

Clarence wrote his letters to Floy on beautiful stationery cards he collected.

RATION BOOKS ▼

621188 AF
UNITED STATES OF AMERICA
OFFICE OF PRICE ADMINISTRATION
4
WAR RATION BOOK FOUR

The government introduced ration stamps during World War II to handle supply shortages. Items such as gasoline, sugar, meat, eggs and even cigarettes all had ration stamps.

Clarence and Floy in 1943.

Clarence and Floy Falstrom

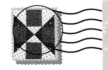

Rifle
Instruction

May 10, 1945

Dearest Floy,

Today was my day at the hospital, so from there I came on into Harrisburg. I sent a Mother's Day card home since they are nicer here than at camp. After one day of sunshine, the rain returned and today it hasn't stopped once. The past three weeks I don't believe we've had over five nice days.

We haven't heard any more about when we leave, although the so-called advance party leaves tomorrow. It may not be until June 1st. In looking on the map, the straight line distance is 815 miles from Fort Jackson to Kansas City, and 930 miles from Harrisburg. However, the travel time, no doubt, would be longer from there. I look for us to be very busy, but I am going to try for rifle instructions there. It will be mostly outdoors, but summer is coming and I expect to be out before winter sets in. Even so, winter shouldn't be so bad there.

I received your Sunday letter this morning. I wonder why Mrs. Cameron can be like she is. Just forget it, she'll get over it sometime and eat you up when she does. Dan has told me he thinks she is off a little in the head. Too bad he has to have such a person for a wife. Religion causes people to put up with difficulty sometimes. If I see definitely that no furlough is coming after we get to the new place, I'll have you down, provided there is a place to stay. The South is supposed to be hard to find a place.

Love,
Clarence

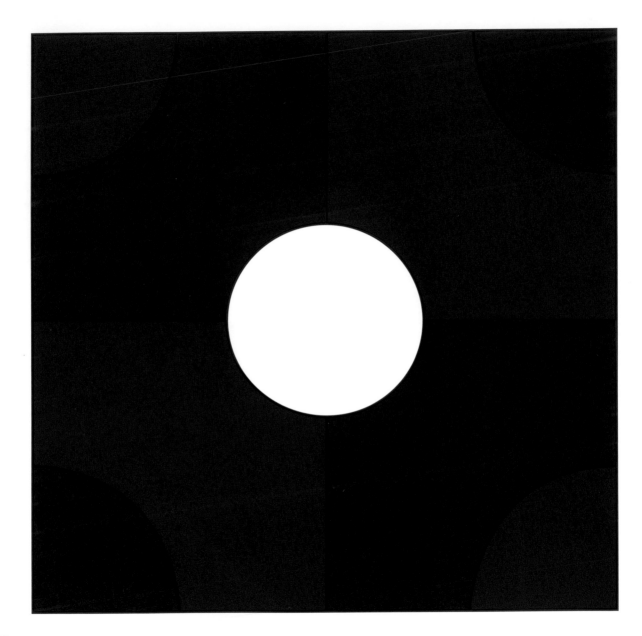

Clarence and Floy Falstrom

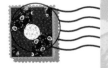

7,000 to 10,000 Men Ready

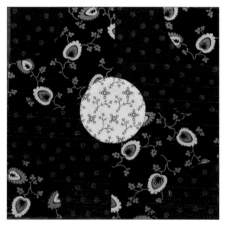

May 14, 1945

Dearest Floy,

We were hooked for both yesterday and today, which is no surprise, after doing almost nothing all week. It seems like it never fails to happen. We haven't heard any more news about when we leave, although about 35 left for Carolina on Friday.

Yesterday I received two letters from you. I saw the picture, *The Valley of Decision*, which was very good. The setting is in Pittsburgh, Pennsylvania. Be sure and see it when it comes there. I haven't heard any more about the furlough, and it's still possible that I may get it at any time. It will be a miracle if I do get it very soon. There is so little to write about when we are tied in that I feel like I should quit trying. I'll resume later.

May 18, 1945 (continued)

I received a letter from you today. We are very busy again now. It looks like one of those long hard spells with no time off like last February and March. We worked until 10:15 p.m. Saturday and until 10:30 last night. There are about 7,000 to 10,000 men to get ready as soon as we can. It looks like no time whatsoever off for a while, then I suppose we'll go to Carolina for a reward.

This morning they sent around a questionnaire asking whether we want to stay until the end of the war. You know what my answer was. I guess you've read about the point system. It takes 85 and I only have 18, so I will have to get out under an age bracket system. I feel they will lower the age before so very long. If you don't hear from me regularly, think nothing of it because we will be very busy.

Love,
Clarence

Clarence and Floy Falstrom

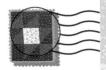

May 24, 1945

The Latest Rumor

Dearest Floy,

I received your letter telling about the tree blowing down. On that hill I don't suppose we'll ever have a lot of luck with trees, but it will have to blow hard to get every tree. I'll plant more when I get home again. I don't expect to be in a whole lot longer now. I'll be 38 in 10 more weeks. I would like to be there during the summer, though.

Last night we worked until 10:00 and will again tonight, Friday and maybe Saturday. We certainly don't get much time off in this work. The latest rumor is that we will leave from June 10 to the 15th. My furlough will be some time away at that rate. No one is even given a three-day pass now. The best thing about the job is no guard duty except the alert guard. It had to be eliminated, until we reached the new camp at least.

I mailed the package today with a jacket, shirt and three hats. If I'm in by fall, I'll write and have them sent back. Sure hope I get the furlough before then. I've learned to never count on a thing, however.

I received a letter from Ma, which was a surprise. When you get in this Army, you learn fast no one seems to care to write. Other fellows say the same things. New people I've met are about the only ones who write me regularly. Maybe you can come for a visit when we get to the new place, but everyone says a place to stay there is almost impossible. If we accidentally get off this week, I'm not sure where I'll go, although I'm invited to New York and also Johnstown, Pennsylvania. After all, it costs to go around, so I can't just go flying everywhere. I still have five rolls of film, so I have plenty of that. When we get to Carolina, I want to make a trip to Florida. It should be nice for pictures. I'll keep you posted on when we leave, etc.

Love,
Clarence

Clarence and Floy Falstrom

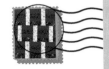

May 30, 1945

The Worst Is Over

Dearest Floy,

This morning I received your letter and five others. I must reread them again this evening. Yesterday was very cloudy, so didn't get any pictures taken. I'm going to mail you several boxes of pictures to look at. Just keep them home. Whenever the ones I sent in May 20th come, send them to me, provided I'm in a permanent place. We are expected to leave here anywhere from June 3 to June 10, but it can't be depended on, like everything else here.

We put in a lot of hours last week. So far this week we haven't worked nights but may at any time. I have CQ for this coming Saturday night, so it may be my chance to go to Hershey on Sunday. I still have about seven pictures left on the roll in the camera, the first ten are pictures of New York.

Today was a very nice day after a downpour yesterday. The furlough must definitely be off until we reach Carolina, so the sooner we get there the sooner I'll get it. There is a rumor that Truman has recommended those over 35 be released, so it may not be so much longer for me at that. I saw Anderson when he came through here but paid no attention to him. He never said much to me. He thought he was so important at Reynolds last summer. I have seen several go who thought they were set. A fellow, Boynton, shook hands and told me goodbye when he heard I was 211111. He was 311111 but he is in Germany. I had to laugh about two hours after he shook hands. He came out on orders himself. They don't look so important when they go through here. All the steam is gone. Anderson might as well expect to be there for some time. I feel like the worst is over and I'll be home before so very long.

Love,
Clarence

Clarence and Floy Falstrom

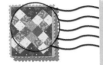

June 1, 1945

We Are Even Rationed

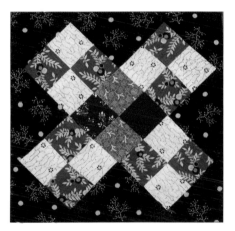

Dearest Floy,

I received your last Thursday's letter today. I suppose by now you have received all the pictures. Saturday evening passed by without much of anything to mention. There were a few phone calls, so had a quiet evening. The radio has some good music on it, too.

The lady who managed the dress shop in Youngstown was made manager of a store in Johnstown. She had invited me down several times, but I never got around to it until yesterday afternoon. It was my only chance before leaving here. She runs a very nice store, you should have seen all the nice dresses. It is a pretty classy store. I only got to be there about eight hours. We ate supper and then went to a show. The day was very stormy looking, so didn't get any pictures.

We are scheduled to leave here next week. Send me some cigars when I get to the new place. We are even rationed on them but have had none at the PX in a week. Smoking a pipe is pretty tiresome.

Love,
Clarence

Clarence and Floy Falstrom

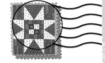

Shipment of 917 Men

June 5, 1945

Dearest Floy,

    By this time next week we should be on our way to the new place, but anything could happen. We even hear a rumor we will go to Fort Dix. That would be too good to be true. Carolina doesn't appeal to me, but at least I'm waiting on time. I received a letter from Linnea today. This talking in here sure ruins letter writing.

    Last night I saw a very funny picture, *Don Juan Quilligan*. The fellow in it sure gets in a mess. Today we sorted old clothing. I got about 100 shoulder patches and also found a new fountain pen in a pocket and a camera trip release.

    The weather still continues to be very cool, you could call it cold. I'm using three blankets to sleep with. Even then it is cold. Linnea sent me five dollars, but she should keep her money. We don't know if we'll get away this weekend. Tomorrow we start on a shipment of 917 men. That will take time, and tomorrow is Thursday The lights are about to go out so must stop here.

Love,
Clarence

Clarence and Floy Falstrom

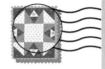

June 10, 1945

New York Pictures

Dearest Floy,

The weather was so bad yesterday and today that I didn't go anywhere. I guess we will leave here about Tuesday, so I will need some of my money for that. If we like, we can travel separately. That way we pay our own fare and they pay us back later. I signed to go that way, but may have to go by troop train. They give us three days to get there, so it may be an opportunity to get a few pictures if weather permits. I'm sure glad I went to Hershey when I did.

This morning the letter came saying you received the second roll of New York pictures. Who the "chick" was I can't say. I don't remember one getting in my way, although several tried to get me to take their picture. When you have a camera people really notice you. The one picture is a florist window on Broadway. On 5th Avenue I saw Max Schling's floral shop. It was beautiful but the sun wasn't in the right direction. You could take the slides down and have Tony show them on his machine. I'll bring mine home when I come. If it is shipped it may get broken and the parts may not be available. I have three rolls of film now and will get another tomorrow. I have used a lot lately, four rolls, and it does run into money. In Harrisburg I bought a roll of black and white, the first I've seen in a year.

I don't know just what route I'll take to Carolina, but have a good map on hand. They give us $27 for the trip. It is more than enough. They give us $9 for three days' meals and the other $18 comes later, possibly 1 to 2 months. I have $25.50 now, so will make out okay, I think. Another fellow and I intend to hitchhike part or most of the way. As soon as we get there I'm trying for the furlough. I still have $35 put away for it. I think our address there will be the same except, of course, for the camp and city, but I'll write you what it is.

Love,
Clarence

Clarence and Floy Falstrom

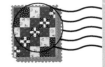

Clean up Barracks

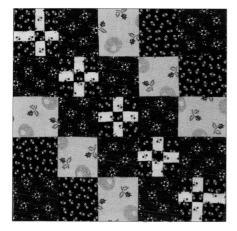

June 14, 1945

Dearest Floy,

I received your Sunday's letter today. I guess this is my last to you from the camp. They gave us our nine dollars for three days' meals today. We leave tomorrow sometime after we clean up these barracks. I went to the dentist Monday, Tuesday and today. My gums have been bleeding a little so thought I had better see about it. While they were at it I got a good cleaning job, so my teeth look very good again. It also got me out of a lot of dirty moving work at the same time. The moving here hasn't caused as much work as Reynolds because this camp is to be used as a separation center for discharges. The move at least means I'm closer to my furlough now, so maybe it won't be much longer.

I saw a sad accident tonight. A woman driver attempted to make a left turn and an MP on a motorcycle hit the car. He was thrown over the top of the car and landed on his back. He remained conscious but was hurt pretty much. The woman was almost hysterical but later on tried to say it was his fault. My name was taken as a witness, but I don't know what will be done about it.

On the way down I hope to get a few pictures, but it will have to depend on the weather. It continues to be cloudy and sultry the past two days. Mine and your letters will be delayed, so if you don't hear from me for a few days, you will know why.

Love,
Clarence

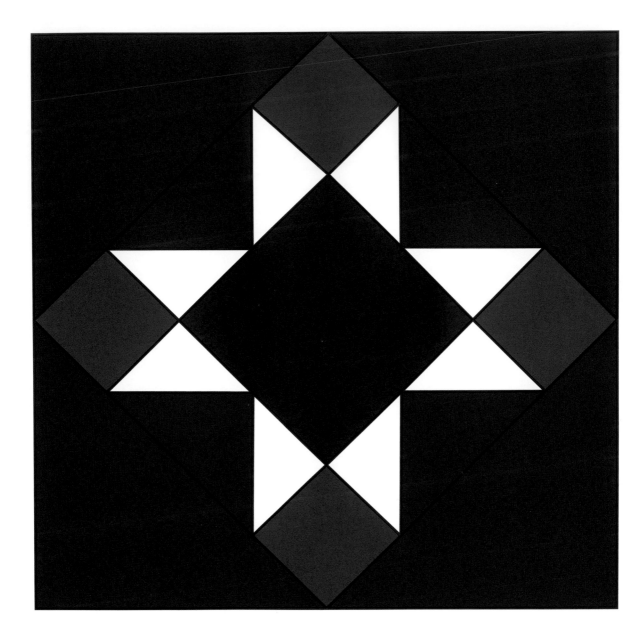

Clarence and Floy Falstrom

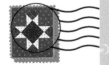

Emergency Furlough

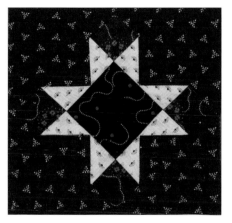

August 3, 1945

Dearest Floy,

The truck job is over and I'm thankful for that. Monday, Tuesday and Wednesday I didn't do a thing. A roster came out for us to go to the range. My dates were the 9th, 10th and 11th of August. A fellow who was scheduled for today, Friday and Saturday had to go leave on an emergency furlough, so since I was about to go nuts doing nothing, I asked the captain if I could go in his place. He said I could so have my first day in and although it was very hot, it is some interest to me. We will fire for record Saturday. I've never fired this particular rifle, but it's supposed to be better than the one used at Crowder.

There is some sort of change about to take place here, so I may not have the same address long, although we stay here in this camp. Your package hasn't arrived yet. I received cards from your folks and Trella, which I appreciated very much.

I saw a very good picture this evening, Irene Dunne in Over 21. Be sure to see it when it gets there, although it will be some time yet. I don't know where I go from here, but I'm so thankful that truck job ended. I see your bank paper lists me as a sergeant; that should be corrected to read "ex-truck driver."

Love,
Clarence

Clarence and Floy Falstrom

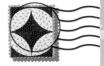

Sergeant of the Guard

August 10, 1945

Dearest Floy,

We move tomorrow to our new company. Last night I served as a sergeant of the guard. I got very little sleep so slept almost all day today. The weather has actually cooled off for a day so is pretty nice now.

I inquired about the package, but no sign of it as yet. The great change in the war may mean releases being given before so very long. Surely things will get better before long. I don't intend doing any more than I possibly need to get by on.

Guess you were surprised to see Dow again. He has his fill of the Army at last, I guess. What our job will be in the new company is hard to know, but right now no one is hurting himself. But we are all getting fed up on it all. Maybe I'll be home sooner than it looks like right now. This is only the first part of August, so I could make it before cold weather comes. Saw a color movie on Bryce Canyon and Zion National Park. It's beautiful.

Love,
Clarence

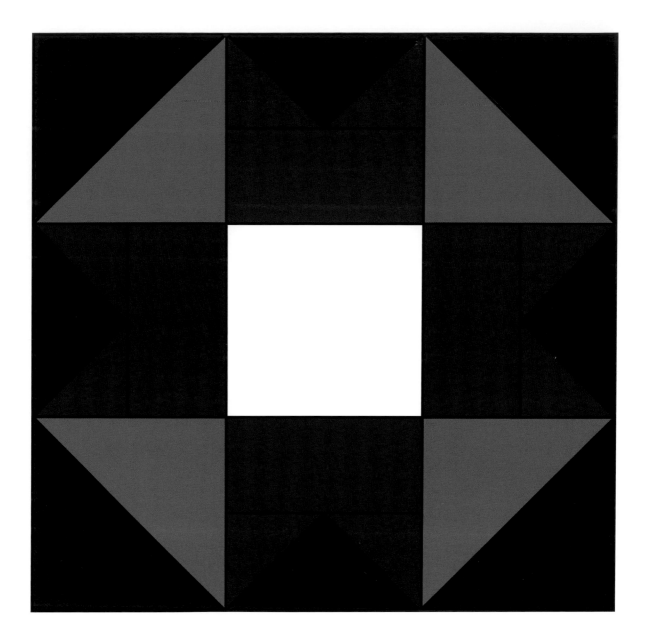

124

Clarence and Floy Falstrom

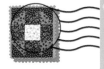

August 14, 1945

Dearest Floy,

The announcement of the end of the war has just come in. This is the day many have waited for. The past three days have almost made a wreck of me in anticipation. I was in Columbia this afternoon but came back at five o'clock. They are giving us a half a day a week off now.

I went into the Carolina Power Company and had a very interesting talk with a big shot there. He showed me pictures of their three plants and all. I didn't do much in town. There isn't anything of interest there and it rained quite a bit. We should see some big changes now, and they can't come too soon. As long as we can get out of Carolina, I can stand to wait a little. I hope to see you again before very long.

August 17, 1945 (continued)

By now you have read the good news about releasing those over 38. I heard it on the radio twice last night and it is in the morning paper. We are now waiting for the War Department Circular, which is the authority for making application. Everyone is very happy about it. We have several who are over 38.

I tried to call you on the phone last night, but there was too much traffic on the lines. I was there from 7:30 to 11:00 p.m., but the tie-up was Chicago. When to expect to get out is a question. I would guess it will be at least another month.

Love,
Clarence

The End of the War

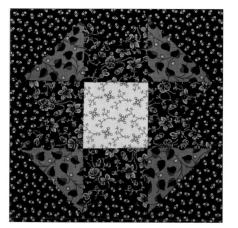

Marie Booker and Wyndom L. Brown

Marie Booker was born in Virginia on June 27, 1924. She began writing letters to Wyndom L. Brown, a private in the United States Army, during World War II. Marie was 20 years old and still in school when she wrote the letters to Wyndom. She often told Wyndom about her school activities, school dances and her friends.

Wyndom L. Brown was born in 1924 in Los Angeles, California. He enlisted in the Army on August 21, 1944 at the age of 20. After the service, Wyndom returned to Los Angeles and lived there his entire life. He died on January 14, 2004 at the age of 80.

Not much is known about Marie Booker after she graduated. She went on to work for the Harris Company's chain of department stores in California and continued to write letters to Wyndom until 1949. Marie died on November 18, 1992 at the age of 73.

U.S. Army-Issued Sewing Kit

Marie Booker

Marie's graduation photo along with a collection of letters she wrote to Wyndom.

An example of a victory sewing thimble manufactured during World War II.

This photograph of a young soldier was recovered from Marie's things. Though the portrait is unnamed and unsigned, it is believed to be that of Wyndom Brown, the gentleman with whom Marie shared a wartime correspondence.

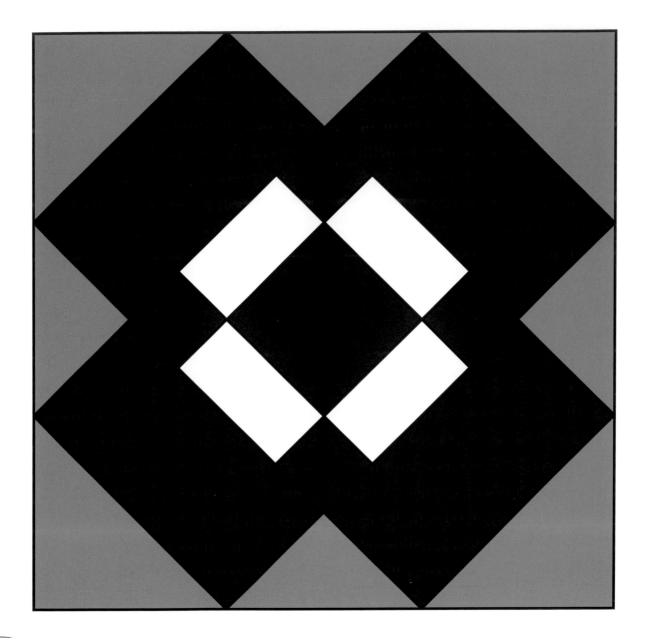

Marie Booker and Wyndom L. Brown

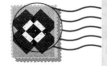

January 5, 1945

Send Me a Picture

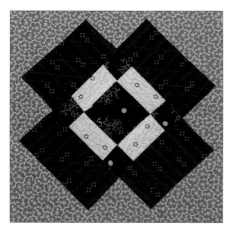

Dear Wyndom,

Sorry I am not using ink as I write this letter. I'm stealing time in class. How have you been? I still have a cold, but I am much better. I was surprised to hear from you and also very glad. About the funny book, my little sisters and brother can't get their work done for looking at the book. Smile. I have only read two stories. I think they have read them all. The life book, I haven't read it yet. My teacher keeps passing by my desk. Smile. I might write the sentence a dozen times, but my teacher looks going past my desk.

I went home from school today, I made it home at eight o'clock. The trip was long and tiresome. The family were all glad to see me. Don't forget to send me the picture. I think you are such a fine and swell person. You seem different from the other soldiers. Of course everyone is different, but your different stands out more than others. I had more fun with you the short hours we were together. I mean Oretha, you and myself.

I also received the picture cards. They are very nice. No doubt this is a short letter, but time is limited now. I will do my best to be a good secretary.

Sincerely,
Marie

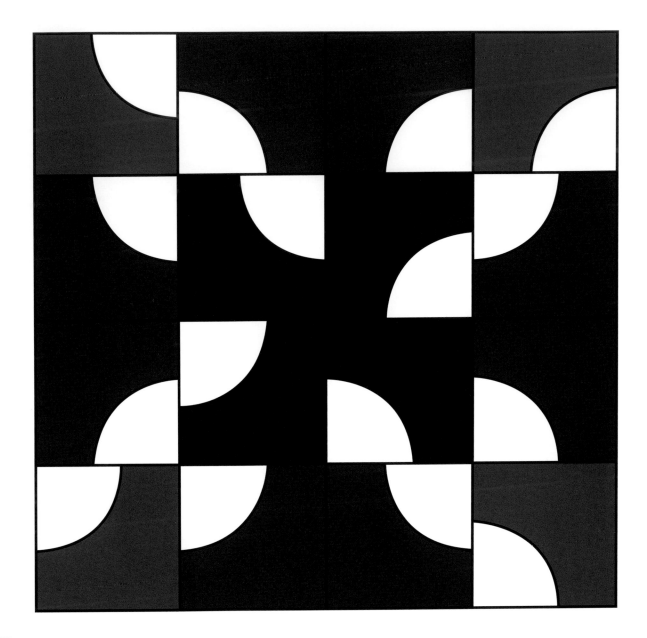

Marie Booker and Wyndom L. Brown

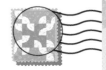

January 21, 1945

Simply Beautiful

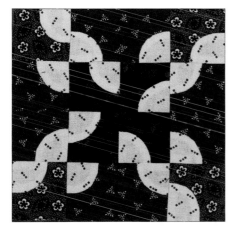

Dear Wyndom,

    I must tell you I was indeed glad to receive your letter. It made me so happy to receive mail from you (my boss). Well, I think that is something. How are you? I am fine and truly hope you are likewise. The family sends their best regards. As for your penmanship in your letters, I think it is simply beautiful. I showed the printing to my three pals and they indeed admired it so. I see now I am going to like my boss. Smile.

    I also received the pictures. I think they all turned out fine. No kidding, I am so sorry I broke the camera. Okay, I will send my part of the money, this is the reason why I hadn't answered any sooner. I had to get the money together. Then after I received it, I didn't know if I should ship it or not. So I thought I would wait a few days longer. I'm enclosing the money in this letter, that's if I don't forget to put it in. Smile.

    California has finally received cold weather. A person almost froze going to school. Every morning the ground looks like blankets of snow. But it isn't snow, it is frost instead. You know yourself how cold frost is.

    Friday, January 19, I went to see Duke Ellington. I think he plays pretty fine music. This week is final exams. I know they are really hard and I am doing my best to make a passing grade, just so I can be your secretary. Don't worry, you won't be sorry if you hire me for your secretary.

    Always,
    Marie

P.S. I am afraid my boss will have to send his secretary stamps for the time being.

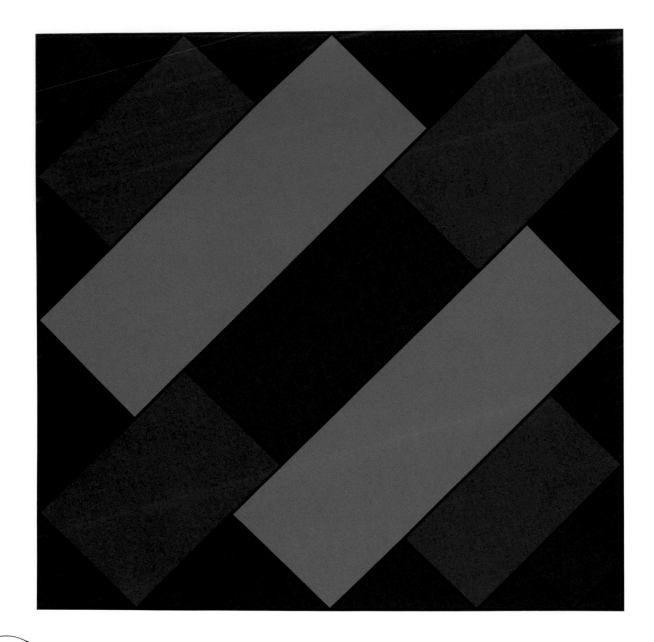

Marie Booker and Wyndom L. Brown

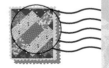

January 24, 1945

Sock and Toe Dance

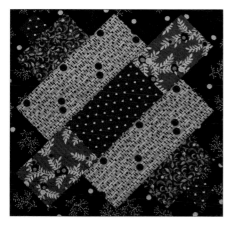

Dear Wyndom,

This is a pleasure to address these few lines to you. How have you been lately? I am fine, also the family. I truly hope you are likewise. I received your letter a week ago. I suppose I was too lazy to answer it right away. And there wasn't any news around town (as if there is some now). Smile.

The family sends their best regards. The weather here is very funny. To me it looks like snow, but that might be only my imagination.

Oh yes, the news, I went to a sock and toe dance at school where you take your shoes off at the door and dance in your stockings and on your toes. But my feet hurt me so much after the dance. I was so glad to get home and jump into bed. I think you can imagine how my feet felt. Smile.

Today at school the principal had a list of students who will graduate. There weren't any colored on the list. Tuesday night my mother gave a social gathering at our home. I was also included in their party. I received a letter from Oretha lately, she told me of the fun you two had after I left. Smile. I think Oretha is a swell kid. When I came to Hollywood that was the first time I had ever seen her. You see, we used to correspond with one another for the last five years, so therefore, it seems as though we had known each other forever. I am sorry, the bell is ringing. Write more next time.

Your secretary,
Marie

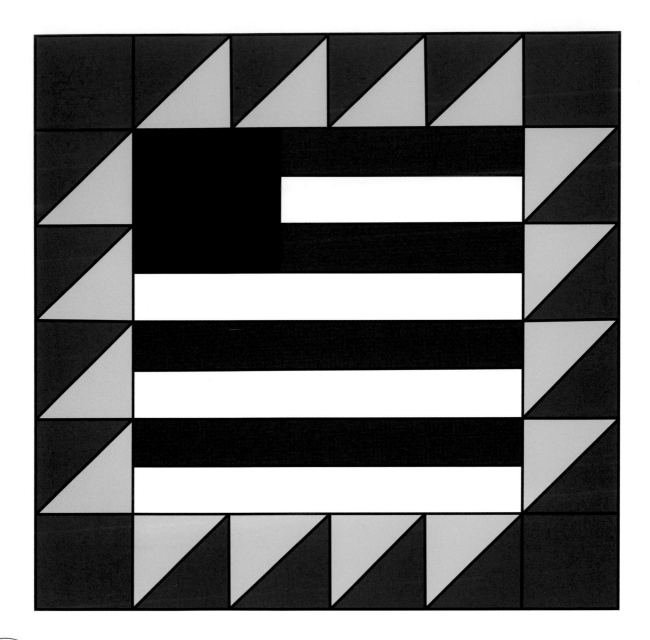

Marie Booker and Wyndom L. Brown

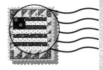

February 9, 1945

Camp in Oakland

Dear Brown,

True enough it has been ages since I last wrote. I remember the new address you gave, but to be truthful, I didn't know that there was a camp in Oakland. I made a mistake by not writing. I should have written sooner, but I am always putting off doing something. Smile.

From the way you started in your letter, you must have had a lonely trip. I suppose you were more than glad to get back to sunny California. How do you like it out there? I was in the Valley about 2½ weeks ago, and while I was there, I went to the neighboring town including Oakland. I don't like it. Maybe my boss is a little different. Smile. You're not so very far from home. How nice. I haven't heard from Oretha in a pretty good while now. But I know they are all well.

The weather here is very nice. I will have more to say in the near future.

Sincerely,
Secretary Marie

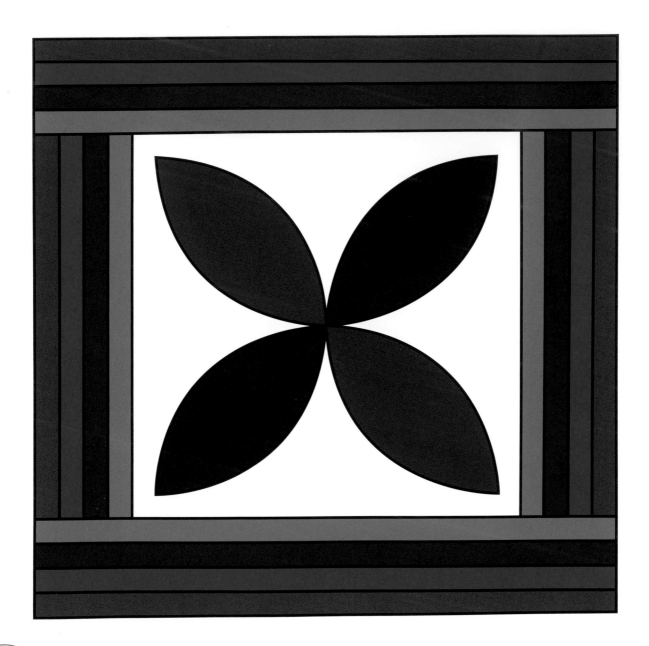

Marie Booker and Wyndom L. Brown

Latest Bands

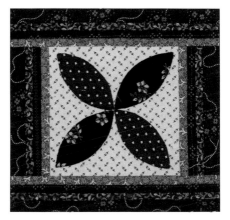

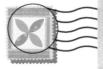

March 6, 1945

Brown,

It was, indeed, a surprise to hear from you. I often wondered why you haven't answered my letter, but until I heard from you, I never knew why. Very glad to hear from you. Your letter finds me well and I sincerely hope my letter finds you the same.

Well, here is that old conversation about the weather. It was nice up until two days ago. Somehow it just up and changed. I know what to do next time, store some good weather up for the cold weather. Smile.

By the way, not many of the latest bands have been up here. I'm still going strong with my recreation activities. This Friday the club is giving a dance. We are all expecting a big crowd with 15 neighboring towns representing. Hope it is a gallant affair.

I'm still working it out in school. It is just so far away from home. Well I'm afraid I have to close, but until I hear from you, I remain.

Yours Always,
Marie

Marie Booker and Wyndom L. Brown

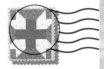

March 14, 1945

USO at Camp Beale

My Dearest,

Your letter was received on time and it found me in the best of health, studying pretty hard. I trust that my letter will find you in the very best of health and enjoying the summer weather. When your letter was received we were enjoying summer weather, but the last few days our weather has changed back to winter.

Last Sunday the USO from Fresno was invited to Camp Beale. My girlfriend and I were also invited. We really had a nice time. I'm glad you joined the M.P. You are so far away, but yet it isn't far at all. We are off for a week for Easter and I'm planning on going to Los Angeles. Maybe, perhaps you will have a furlough around Easter. At least we hope so. Smile.

My studies are getting pretty hard, and I have little time for writing, but I will try to do my best by not letting my letters stay too long without answering them. Received a letter from Jerry and she said she is planning on going to school. But I'm afraid she will have to wait until next term. Wyndom, I'm so sorry I have to close. Until I hear from you I remain.

Forever Yours,
Marie

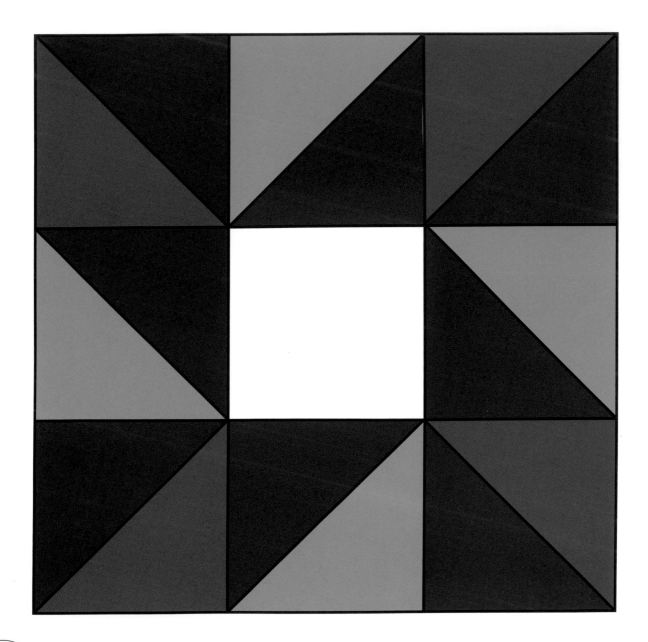

Marie Booker and Wyndom L. Brown

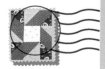

Navy Supply Depot

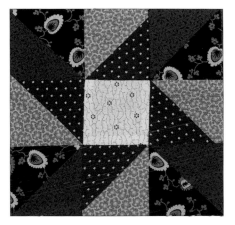

April 15, 1945

Dear Wyndom,

I'm sorry that I waited as long as I did before answering your letter. My school studying is rather busy, and last week my throat had given me trouble. But at present, I'm feeling fine and hope to return to school soon.

The family sends their best regards and give your family the same. I see you are rather busy yourself. Looks like the rate you're going you soon won't be able to take so much of working and studying at the same time.

Did you have a nice Easter? Mine was fine. Oh yes, you asked how is my girlfriend from Oakland? She is fine, she also has a new car now. She is still working at the Navy Supply Depot. She said that in July they will start laying them off. They lay off again and again, they might not keep her.

Things around Tulare are about the same except that they are building a new café here and we have a very good ball team. So far they have won all their games. Roy Milton, Billy Eckstine and S. King have been in Fresno the last month and a half. I'd say between Milton and Eckstine, Milton was much better. I didn't attend S. King.

The weather here is very warm. I can say we're having an early summer this year. Well, I'm sorry I have to close. Until I hear from you, I remain.

Yours Always,
Marie

Marie Booker and Wyndom L. Brown

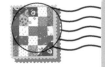

April 18, 1945

A Weekend Pass

Dear Wyndom,

Hi, how have you been lately and always? I am okay and I sincerely hope my letter finds you likewise. I am writing in the cool of the evening of April 18th. Today, and the other days, have been very warm. I started a letter in school today but it was just too hot to finish.

I enjoyed the cards very much. Yes, I think San Francisco is a nice city. But it is too big for me. I like a small town like Vallejo. I seem to like Berkeley fairly well, but Oakland, I don't know nothing about it.

Glad you had a nice Easter. Too bad you didn't get a weekend pass so you could really thoroughly enjoy your Easter.

My, you write such cute letters. I really get a thrill out of reading them. Smile. Okay, I will send you a picture, but as the old saying goes, I don't have any at present. I would also like to have a billfold-size picture of you, now how about that? I know when you receive this letter you will be back at the barracks. I know all the tents were plenty cold.

That'll be fine if you have a good chance of being stationed here, I mean, in California. I saw *Hollywood Canteen* a few Sundays back and I think it was grand. It was playing in Hollywood while I was there last year. Just think, it is just now getting to Tulare. *The Birth of a Star* is here. I heard it was good, so if my brother comes by, I will go.

We have a carnival in town now. I suppose I will go one night and just see how it is. Well, I will close. And will you give me permission to do so? Thank you.

Always,
Marie

Marie Booker and Wyndom L. Brown

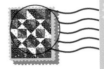

Reading Your Mail

April 26, 1945

Dear Wyndom,

   Yours was received and it found all well. I sincerely hope mine will find you the same. The family sends their best regards. The weather here is lovely, hope your part of the country is the same. Will you bear with me for a little while, while I type this letter to you? You can see I need some more practice and that is just what I'm doing. I hope you will try not to look too much at all the mistakes because there are so many.

   Usually when I try to type a letter, I can't think of much to say. And this is the same way. I have only five more minutes to go before the bell will ring and I'm just beginning this letter. My, your letter sure was interesting. I sure did get a thrill out of reading your mail. You can think of so many things to say, while I can think of so little.

   My sister from Vallejo came down Saturday and we had a very nice time together. She stayed two days with us. She had to be back at her job the following Tuesday. Please excuse a short letter, I am sure I can think of more to say in the near future.

                    Always,
                    Marie Booker

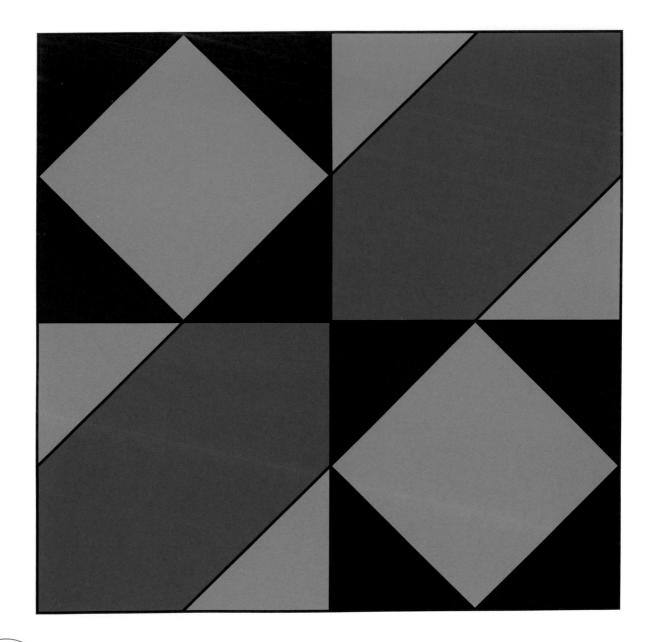

Marie Booker and Wyndom L. Brown

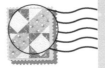

May 2, 1945

Really Be Careful

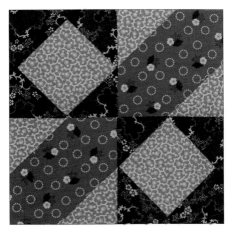

Dear Wyndom,

Yours was received some time ago, which found all well. I sincerely hope mine will find you the same. No doubt you will have wondered what became of me. I'm still going to school and my school activities keep me pretty busy. These last few weeks have kept me so busy, but my last five weeks are really going to keep me working.

The weather is agreeable here. The family sends their best regards. For Easter I spent a lovely and perfect week in L.A. and Hollywood. I saw all my relatives and friends and they showed me a lovely time. The only downside was that the week was too short. Smile.

Now you tell me about yourself. I haven't been to any recent dances, therefore I don't know anything along that line. The West Coast Relays will be held in Fresno this year and I am going. It will be great with all the fellows back.

Now, I want you to be really careful, because in your next letter I wouldn't want to hear of you being in the hospital. So please be careful. No answer soon.

Forever Yours,
Marie

Marie Booker and Wyndom L. Brown

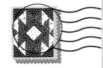

May 22, 1945

West Coast Relays

Dear Wyndom,

I take great pleasure in addressing you these lines. When my letter reaches you, I hope it finds you okay. I know you're wondering why I haven't written before now. Due to all my school activities, I have been slower than I thought I would be. I hope that you can find room in your heart to forgive me. To tell you the truth, I have been a busy person. I sincerely hope you'll believe me on this.

No doubt when I tell you I was in your fair city two weeks ago, you will wonder why I didn't let you know. It wasn't like I didn't have the time to tell you, this all happened so suddenly. I was a delegate for the B.Y.P.U. (Baptist Young People's Union) at a church convention. I did enjoy myself. I went a few places while being there. I was there 2½ days. The convention was swell. It was held on 12th and Willow Street.

There isn't much news around Tulare. Last Saturday I attended the West Coast Relays, and my, they were grand. I did enjoy every moment of all the activities that took place. Fresno's Edison High School sure did good. There were so many people there.

There has been one dance in Fresno since I wrote you, but I didn't attend. I have only a few more days of school, then school vacation for a while. I have planned to attend college so far in life.

I couldn't have found a better friend than you when we met. Though our meeting was strange, we did enjoy every moment of it. You are what I call a friend and also a close one.

Well Wyndom, I know you must sure be tired, so I will close.

Always,
Marie

Marie Booker and Wyndom L. Brown

Dangerous Job

June 30, 1945

Dear Wyndom,

   Again I take the greatest pleasure in addressing these few lines of happiness. Well dear, I am in Oakland, and I will be for a while. Then perhaps I might go to Vallejo. You see, I have a brother and sister there. My sister is working out where you are stationed. I have planned to go to Vallejo tomorrow, but it will only be for awhile. I am staying with my girlfriend, so I won't set a date when I will see you, but I wanted you to know when you can see me. You do have a dangerous job, all I can say is be really careful. Also, when I return from Vallejo, I will put in for a job. I don't like cold weather any more than you do.

   We arrived Sunday and it sure was tiresome. I sincerely hope when you see me, I won't be looking like I am now. My face is swollen and my hands are, too. I should say one arm is likewise. Nothing too bad, just the bedbugs got a hold of me. My hand is hurting, so therefore I will close.

Yours Always,
Marie

Carter O. Lilly and Genny N. Brun

Carter O. Lily was born in West Virginia in 1914. He met Genny N. Brun, a student at Phoenix, Arizona's St. Mary's Catholic High School, in a park one day during a furlough. The two began a correspondence shortly thereafter.

Carter wrote Genny (whom he called "Ginny") weekly letters while he was stationed in San Diego, California, signing all his correspondence with the name *Red*. The two often talked about meeting up and going on a date after the war was over, but according to Genny's family, they don't believe it ever happened.

Carter returned to Virginia after the war and died in 1976 at the age of 62. Genny died on April 30, 2010 at the age of 83.

Great Falls Beer-Issued Sewing Kit

Great Falls Beer Company passed out these sewing kits to soldiers. They were very compact, only 2 inches tall, but carried two colors of thread and a compartment for pins and needles, capped off by the thimble.

Genny at age 19, when she was writing her letters to Carter.

The Singer Sewing Machine Company distributed Singer Domino cards like the ones pictured here to soldiers during World War II.

Letters that Carter O. Lilly wrote to Genny.

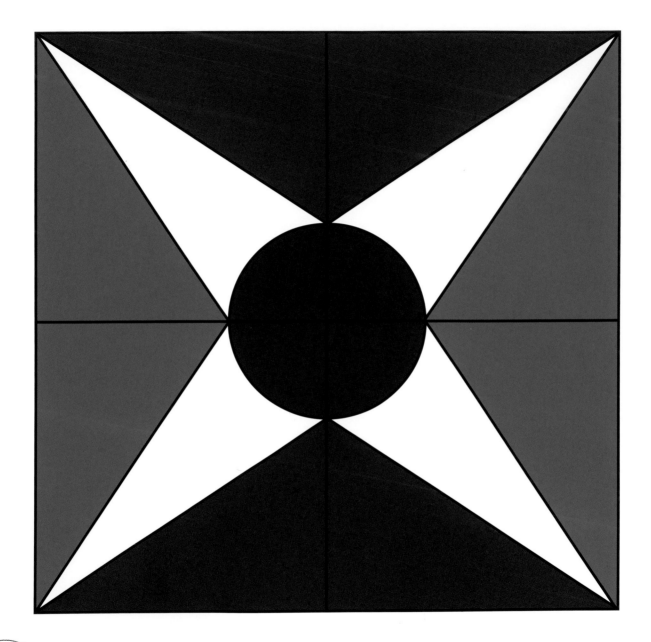

Carter O. Lilly and Genny N. Brun

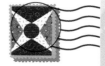

Lost a Battalion

September 3, 1942

Hello Ginny,

I guess you will be surprised to get a letter from me, and maybe you can't even read it, for I don't write very well. I sure wish you could have stayed longer, but I guess you were glad to get home. Well how was the trip? Have any bad luck such as flat tires, etc.? I am sorry that I can't send a picture to you, but I promise to the next time I write. If I get shipped out I will send you a lot of souvenirs from wherever I go. Some of our boys were sent away yesterday and we lost a battalion today.

Maybe you will see the battalion somewhere. If you do, will you please return it to me? Ha ha.

Well, the Army is the same every day, and not knowing you very well, there is very little to write about. In fact, there really isn't anything to interest you.

I promise a more interesting letter soon with some pictures, so write and tell me about your trip home. Make it a real long letter for I sure get lonesome here. I was out on pass last night and had a real nice time, sure wish you could have been with me. So, I will stop for now and let you rest today.

A friend,
Red

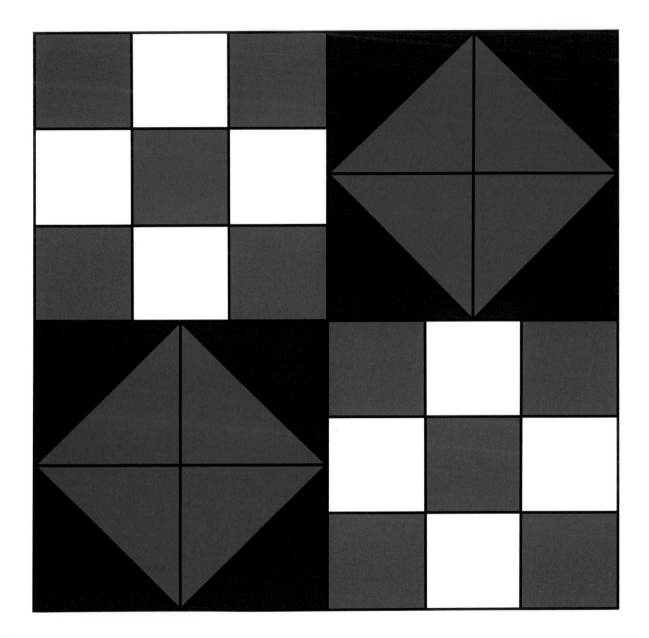

Carter O. Lilly and Genny N. Brun

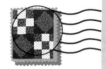

October 11, 1942

Guitar and Mandolin

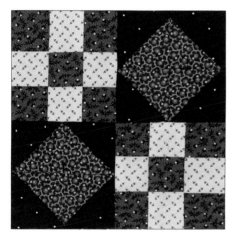

Dear Ginny,

I began to think I would never get to answer your letter, for I leave the site at five o'clock every morning and get back at about 11 o'clock at night. I am driving again, I have about 90 minutes to feed three times daily.

I have a new guitar and mandolin, so we have a fair time here. Say, I'm sort of proud of you for after all, many of the boys don't have a girl so nice to write to. Say, if I can get a two-day pass, I am going to Mexico some weekend if we stay here and I will send you a souvenir. It looks as if I am stuck here until the rest of the battalion leaves. Boy I am sure tired just now, but if I get to sleep good tonight I will be okay.

I will try to write a long letter next time, and I will send you a picture of me if you will promise to not show it to your friends. How about it? Oh yes, I'm awful sorry that you were sick, sure hope you are feeling better by now. If you are not, write as soon as you can, for I will be anxious to hear.

Say Ginny, has your boyfriend gone to the service as yet? I hope not for your sake, but I guess all of us will have to go before we win a war. I am sort of jealous, you know. I will write you as soon as I leave here. Maybe send you a telegram before I go.

I would give anything if you lived here so I could see you sometime. Well Ginny, there isn't any news here, so I can't write much. Guess I will sign off. Please don't feel bad about the pictures I made for you because I can take anything they give me in good heart if you will keep writing to me. So for now, bye-bye.

With all my love,
Red

Carter O. Lilly and Genny N. Brun

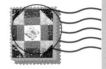

No Lights Here

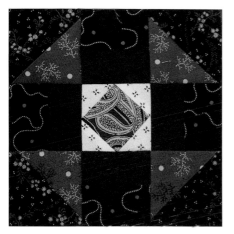

October 13, 1942

Dear Ginny,

I guess you think I am silly but honestly, I just can't seem to wait to get a letter from you. It seems that I certainly look forward to hearing from you. Maybe it does sound silly, but I guess it's just one of those things, so if it gets too bad, I guess you would just have to bawl me out good.

Well today we lost another battalion, so look out for it. How is your school going? I hope you really like it, I would have been better off if I had gone. Maybe then I could read my letters. Well, I have a new guitar now. I wish you could hear me. I don't play very well, but I don't like to play by myself very much. We don't have any lights here, so I am trying to write by a candle and I sleep in a dugout. So, you can see how much your letters help. It is about the only communication I have with civilians.

Have you learned to shoot your gun yet? I hope to get my rifle before long. The president is going to speak in about 20 minutes, I hope I can go somewhere to hear him

I'm back again now. The officer just came around and gave us a gift made by the Red Cross. Well, this is all the paper I have just now, so I guess you are sick of this by now anyways.

As ever a pal,
Red

P.S. Don't keep me waiting for mail too long.

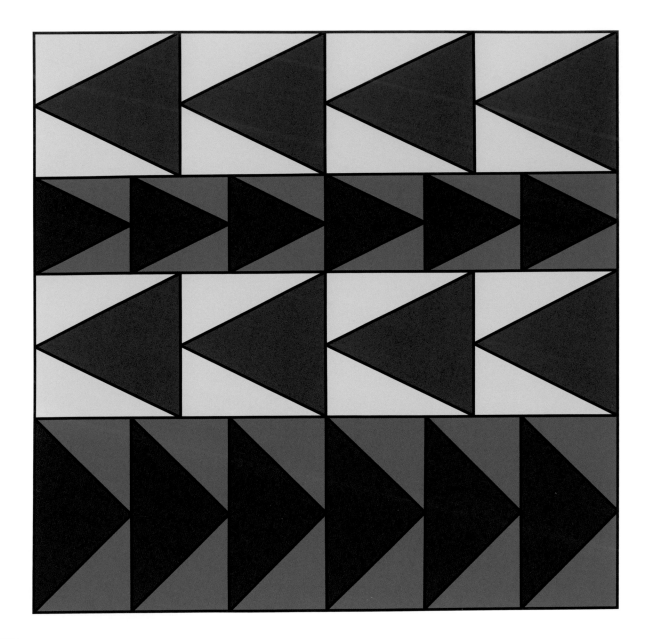

Carter O. Lilly and Genny N. Brun

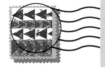

Gas Ration

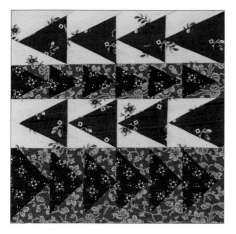

October 15, 1942

Dear Ginny,

I didn't think you had forgotten me, I just thought maybe you are busy. Of course I am always watching for letters from you. Yes, it is just too bad about the gas ration. We can't get out very much now either, about once every 10 days or so. We have to make out the best we can.

We have a bicycle here we ride over to the airport. Believe it or not, we do like to ride it since it's the only way we have to pass the time off.

Well how about the job? I guess it will be fun for you to work in a dimestore through the holidays. And about the pictures of you, I'll bet they are good too, for cameras don't lie and I happen to remember just how you look. I have lost a lot of weight since I met you in the park, but maybe I will be my old self soon.

I'm anxious to see your sister, but I hope your hunch was right and you will get to come out here soon, won't you. Come without telling me, will you? For I am crazy to see you. This is all the time I have just now and there really isn't anything to write, so don't forget the picture. I will get mine for you when I go to town again soon. And call me "buddy" again in your next letter, for I like to be your "buddy." I can hardly wait for your letters.

Red

Carter O. Lilly and Genny N. Brun

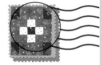

October 24, 1942

Busted to Private

Dear Ginny,

Say, you do write the sweetest letters I have ever read, and by the way, you were just on time this time. I know you won't be very proud of me when I tell you I got busted to private yesterday. If I could see you and talk to you I know you would understand. You see, I was in charge of 10 men here, so I was held responsible for what they each did. I couldn't stay up all the time to keep them awake and the lieutenant caught some of them asleep and broke me. Anyway he called me tonight and said he was going to give my rating back.

Say, you are tops in every way, I bet you are tops in school, too. I think it's a pity you didn't go deer hunting, maybe you will later. This pen won't write, but it is all I have now, so I will try to finish with it. You bet I like the type of music you do, I'm crazy about "My Devotion" and about "Your Bedroom." You just keep what you want in it and that's the best part of life, to be able to have a place of your own to do as you please. Here we can't have anything of our own unless we keep it hid. I have boxing gloves, a guitar, a ball glove and tennis rackets but don't have a place to play tennis. But, we get plenty of time for boxing since the Marines have a company here by us and we usually mix with them.

Yesterday I was the coach out at the rifle range. Had to teach new men how to shoot. I have to go back Friday and Sunday. I'm going to sleep more now since I have lost my rating, I had a chance for discharge but turned it down. I had several years of mining experience and lots of the miners have been sent back to the mines, but honest I would feel like a quitter to go back now.

I will have to close, for there is no more news. If you're angry because I am a bad soldier, I sure will work hard to show you I can earn my stripes back and even more. Write soon, for I can hardly wait to get your mail.

As ever,
Red

Carter O. Lilly and Genny N. Brun

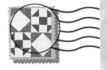

December 14, 1942

Bad for Our Christmas

Dear Ginny,

I just came in from a hard day on the range and found your letter here, so you know I was happy. I don't know of anything better I could have wished for than a nice letter from you. Since I can't see you, I do appreciate your letters, though I do want to see you very, very badly. You do sort of flatter me about my letters.

Oh yes! About my family, I do have a brother. He is a little younger than myself and was shipped out of Washington three months ago, and I haven't heard from him since. I have one older than me, he lives in West Virginia. You see, ever since my mother died when I was nine, I left the rest of the family, so they all seem as strangers would. Yes, you have told me about your family and you should be proud of them, for after all it is not so pleasant all alone.

I would like to see you before I leave here, that way I would make sure I get back. Yes, it was a pity you lost your ride on the plane, but you don't have to make me jealous by telling me who was going to take you. You see I am very jealous, especially about you. Don't laugh either.

Speaking of Christmas shopping, I don't know if I'll get a pass to even go or not, but I hope to anyway, for I want to go so badly. But, we are already on the holiday alert so that looks bad for our Christmas. You see, today I was coaching a battery of men that were leaving the States in a very short time. They were trying their best to learn to shoot real well. Some of them seem glad to go but said they would have liked to have stayed on till after Christmas.

Well Ginny, it is time for me to go on guard, so I will have to sign off for now. I can hardly wait to hear from you.

As ever,
Red

P.S. I just read your letter again. Every time I read it you are a lot sweeter, so don't keep me waiting now.

Carter O. Lilly and Genny N. Brun

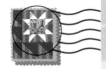

December 22, 1942

The Happiest Soldier

Dear Ginny,

I just got your package and I guess you know I am the happiest soldier in the whole army. But I really am ashamed that I can't get out to send one thing, not even to my people. Say, Honey, I am so awful proud of the picture. I bet I will always keep it, no matter where I go to. You are so sweet to me sometimes, I wonder why. I bet I do make you glad someday that you are so good. I think it is awful that they don't let us at least have one day off to do a little bit of Christmas shopping. Don't you?

I would give 10 years of my life to see you before I leave here. Part of the boys left tonight but they wouldn't tell us where they went. They said the rest of us would be leaving soon after Christmas. Maybe then I can send you a souvenir from the islands, you bet I will if there is a chance.

Ginny, I hope you do have a swell time at Christmas. You know, the boys here all saw your picture and they say they sure would like a girlfriend as pretty as you. So I am a little jealous and won't even let them see it anymore. I hope I have a letter from you in the mail tomorrow afternoon. I would have liked to have met your sister while she was here. Maybe I will sometime.

How much vacation do you get for the holidays? Two weeks or more I hope. What do you think you will do when you finish school? Something interesting and easy I hope.

I can't tell you ever how much I like you for the nice picture and stationery you sent. Honey, I will get out soon and send you a really nice souvenir. For now, bye-bye and thanks one more million times.

Yours forever,
Red

Carter O. Lilly and Genny N. Brun

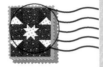

January 25, 1943

The Big Plane

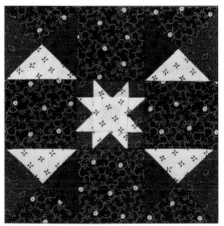

Dear Ginny,

Honey, I got your package today. Boy, oh boy, am I happy now. The medal is so nice and the cookies were the first we have had in ages. But honestly Ginny, I can't go on letting you be so good to me. I have your picture out now where I can write one line then look at you.

Say Ginny. I don't know how to show you my appreciation for everything, but you do make me so awful happy. I just wish every one of the boys had a girlfriend like you. If they did I am sure the war would not last long. You know, I think more of my medal now then I would a new car, and if I can I will get a pass tomorrow and go have your picture made.

I am lonesome for you now. I really want to get this war over. I bet I will see you then if you will let me? Ginny, the big plane that brings the mail in here went through the fence today but didn't do much damage. Say, I keep my gun in perfect shape so it will be nice for you. Yesterday the major asked me how I kept it so nice. If he only knew what I plan to do with it. Maybe he would understand.

Well Honey, I must stop and go on guard so thanks again for everything and be good. I can hardly wait to get a letter from you so don't make it too long. Bye now.

Red

Carter O. Lilly and Genny N. Brun

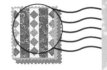

Off Duty

February 7, 1943

Dear Ginny,

I was surprised to get a letter from you today for I really wasn't expecting one. It's so sweet of you. No, I didn't sell my phone. They still want it but won't offer me enough for it. I want you to have it. I guess you will call me silly, but a lot of people would like to have it. When I send it to you, if you don't want it anymore, just smash it so the wrong people can't ever have it.

Honey, I miss you, thanks a bushel for the picture of your little brother and be sure and send a snap of you. You bet you will get a big one of me, but you see we can only get to town about every two weeks so I am awful slow. Gee, I bet it's a pretty place where you live, isn't it? Well I don't know when I will leave, they have told us several times that it will be soon so I never can tell.

Ginny, it's time for me to go off duty now and I just wrote you last night, so for now, bye-bye, Honey. Answer when you can and don't get in bad with your teacher just to write to me.

As ever,
Red

P.S. I will try to mail the phone this week, Honey.

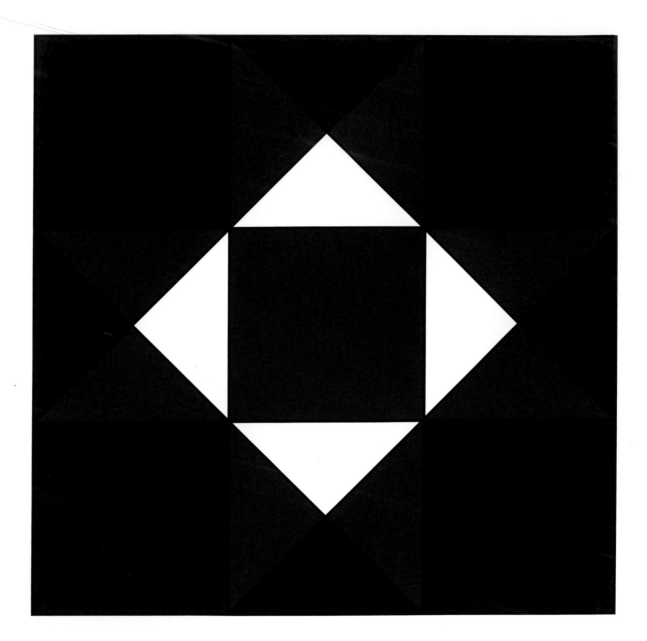

Carter O. Lilly and Genny N. Brun

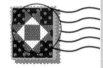

June 17, 1943

Made My Stripes Back

Hello Ginny,

I'm sorry I didn't get to answer your letter last night but I was awful busy. Honey, you sure made me feel awful good when you said you want to see me. But then when you tell me about your dates, it sure hurts me. Well Honey, I won the furlough I told you about with a score of 196 of a possible 200, but I don't know just when I will leave. About the 1st of July, I think.

Do you see, Honey, what a good rifle you are going to get when the war is over? Of course I will have to have it changed into a short gun for you. Well, I made my stripes back yesterday and have a very good chance of a sergeant rating sometime this month. You see, it was a good thing I was transferred, for I never would have done any good with the old outfit.

Ginny, Honey, I would give anything to see you before I go home or soon after. Maybe I will have time to say hello in Phoenix if I decide to go that way, but if it is possible I will get a phone out.

Well Honey, have you gone to work as of yet? I wish you wouldn't. I don't want you to work for some silly reason. You are too darn sweet to work, I have to work pretty hard now since I am first cook and have more men to feed all the time. You bet, Darling, I would like to help you cook dinner if you would teach me how. I bet your cake was good, wasn't it? Send me the recipe and let me try to make it, how about it? It seems the only cake recipe I know how to make is for 300 men, so it would be sort of hard for me to bake a small one. Well, Darling, I must close now and go take a shower for I worked hard today.

Yours now and forever,
Red

Carter O. Lilly and Genny N. Brun

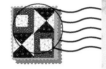

June 28, 1943

Sweetest Girl
I Ever Met

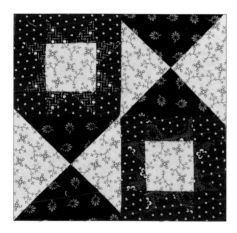

Dear Ginny,

I had a sweet letter from you today. Honest, Dear, you are so sweet. Maybe I will have time to come through your town. I sure would like to. You see, I have a three-day pass. If they will give it to me on my furlough, it will be swell. What have you been doing to pass time, Darling? I just do the same thing over and over again. Today I made biscuits and have to make breakfast tomorrow morning, so I can't write much tonight. Say, my darling, how am I going to do without your letters long enough to go home and back? I sure will miss your letters.

What I want to tell you, Honey, is that I was going to get married when I go home. But, oh! Well, you see, Darling, my most precious one, I love you dear and can't help it. Maybe it is just the sweet letters you write to me, Ginny, but I can't sleep thinking about you. I know this will sound silly to you, so if you don't believe me you don't have to answer, but really I can't help it. I realize you will never love me or like me very well, so I guess we will just have to quit writing so much, for I can't go on like this.

You have been so sweet, and I guess us country boys can't just pass it off like regular guys. But, Darling, you will never know just how I feel about you. Of course it's all my fault because you are the sweetest girl I ever met. Don't feel bad, Darling. Answer if you want to, but that's the way I feel.

Just,
Red

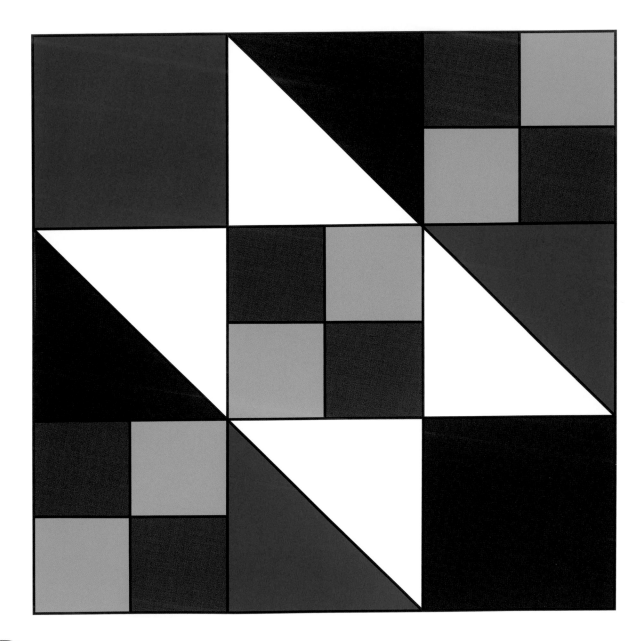

Carter O. Lilly and Genny N. Brun

Drive Me Crazy

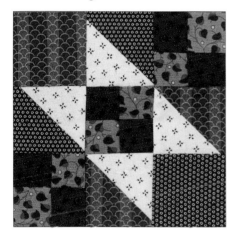

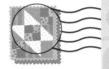

July 23, 1943

Dear Ginny,

Say, what are you trying to do, drive me crazy? No letters in three weeks. You know I can't stand that.

I just got back from furlough in time to get five shots in my arms and boy are they sore.

Honey, believe me that I missed your letters so much while I was home that I couldn't enjoy my trip. My girl was so mad when she found out that I had changed my mind. Maybe she has changed, too. After all, two years is a long time, you know.

Did you miss my letters? Say, what have you been doing anyways? Well, I won't write much more tonight for my darn arm is too sore. Please write me a nice big long letter, will you? I can't wait much longer.

Yours forever,
Red

Carter O. Lilly and Genny N. Brun

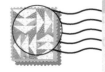

August 17, 1943

So Awful Much

Dear Ginny,

Well, Dear, I really am afraid that you are mad at me now. I just thought that for some reason you didn't want to hear from me anymore, so I just didn't write. You are awful sweet, Honey. I will always keep your cards and letters and above all your medal. I love it, maybe just because you gave it to me. You see, Ginny, I just thought so awful much of you that I could hardly go on the way I was, writing every day, and when I went home to see my girlfriend, I wanted a letter from you so bad that I came back early to see if you had wrote yet. Of course I was disappointed you had not.

Well, Honey, how are you and your boyfriend getting along? Write and tell me? We are having a big dance here tonight. I sure wish you were here. I don't dance very well but I would feel stuck up to dance with you. You see, not very many boys are lucky enough to have girlfriends like you, Dear. Say, I had some pictures made while I was home so I will send you one as soon as they come.

Please send me a snapshot that you had made this summer. Will you? Well, Honey, I am cooking yet and with good luck I should make sergeant. and maybe staff sergeant. in a short time. Well, it's time for lights out so I will say bye-bye for now, Dear.

Red

P.S. What is your favorite number now? Hurry and write, Honey, I will be waiting.

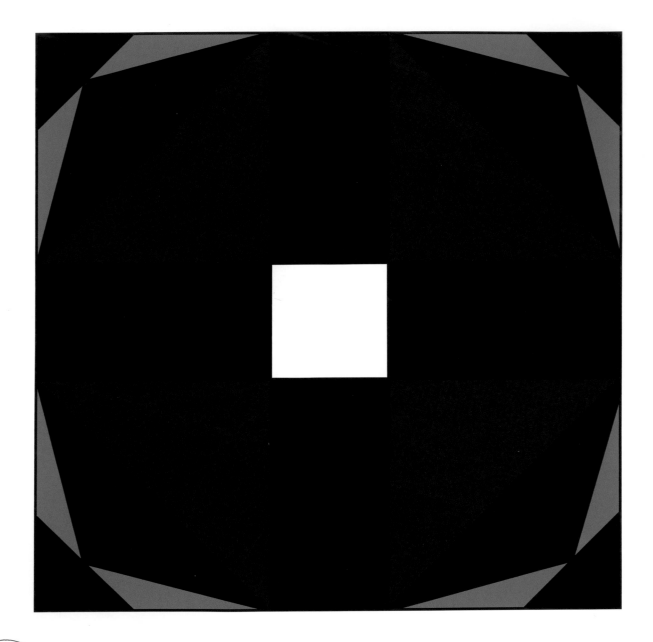

Carter O. Lilly and Genny N. Brun

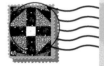

August 26, 1943

Dear Ginny,

Well here I go again. I'm sorry I didn't answer your letter sooner but, Honey, I have been terribly busy. You see, I have to take a first-class gunners test for a sergeant rating, so for two nights I have been reading up on it and today I took the test. I just hope I pass.

Honey, you don't write nice long letters like you did. Do you get bored with my silly letters? Well if you do, I just can't do any better and every word of them is true. I really love your letters and they make me awful lonesome for you, Dear. But honest, I am very jealous about you. You know it really hurts when you write about your boyfriends.

Honey, I really want to see you in the worst way. You're so sweet and fine in every respect. I am so simply crazy about you. Laugh if you want, but it's true. You think you will ever come to South Dakota before school? I would give anything to see you, but I can't come up there.

Well, how is the job by now? Don't you work too hard, and you can take time out to write to me. Can't you? I had a letter from my girl, she wants to come see me but I don't know what to tell her just yet. Oh yes, about three days ago I went out where they were burning a field of grass and caught me a rabbit. I thought about you and wondered if you could have shot it had you been here, Sweetheart. Please write more in your next letter, will you?

Ginny, I wish you would move out here. Do you think you would like living in the East? I believe you could. Well, I am still cooking but took my exam for mess sergeant. Maybe I will make it, I sure hope so. When is your birthday? Tell me in your next letter, will you? Well, I can't think of anything else to write for now so I will say goodnight for the present and hope I dream about you. Send me a big kiss, will you?

Yours forever,
Red

My Girl

Carter O. Lilly and Genny N. Brun

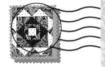

You Are the Sweetest

September 4, 1943

Dear Ginny,

How's my Honey? I hope you aren't as tired as I am. I had a hard day today and have inspection tomorrow. Let me tell you, Sweetheart, just what I did today. I worked in the kitchen until noon today, then I took a shower, and then I washed and ironed five sets of clothes. Do you know anyone that would like to marry a guy like me? I can cook, though not so well, and I can wash, iron, mop floors and all sorts of things.

Say, Honey, you asked me why I didn't want my girlfriend out here. Well here it goes. First of all, I don't know for sure if we would hit it off like we used to, and you see, I don't want to get married until I am out and can make enough money to support her. I don't know just who I want to marry. Say, Honey, of all the girls I know, I'll bet you are the sweetest. I like your letters better anyways. Only they are not as long as they used to be and you don't write very often either.

Well Darling, I have to sew on some sergeant stripes before inspection tomorrow, so I had better say bye before long and go do it. Sweetheart, why don't you write more often? I love your letters. I always carry one with me so I can read it when I feel low, so please write often. Will you Darling? Oh yes, I wanted to know when your birthday is, so tell me please.

Yours,
Red

Carter O. Lilly and Genny N. Brun

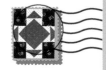

Most Thoughtful Girl

September 21, 1943

Dear Ginny,

How's school? Most of all, how are you? I don't want you to feel bad about school and all, but still, I want you to go. I just hope you will do as well this year as you did last year, and I am sure you will.

Thanks a lot for the nice card you sent. I wish it was you in the picture on the front and that I could be there, too. Honey, I know you are the most sweetest and most thoughtful girl in Arizona. I wish there was some way I could see you. Every day I think about you more and more.

Well, as for me, I am doing okay on my job, but haven't been going out as much lately. Last night we had a dance and I went but it was a flop as usual, too many soldiers. Say, how are you, Darling, with your social life? Only don't tell me about your dates for it makes me jealous. I really mean it, Dear, believe me.

Did you give up your job when you started school? I wish I could go to school at night now. Maybe I will get to go to Army school later if we don't go overseas soon, but I would rather go to war. Well, Honey, I don't have very much time today, so I will sign off for now and write again soon. Answer today if you have time.

Red

Carter O. Lilly and Genny N. Brun

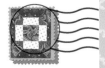

Three Weeks in the Desert

October 28, 1943

Dear Ginny,

Just came in from three weeks in the desert so I will write you first. Ginny, I miss your letters. How was the housekeeping you and your girlfriends did? I hope you had a swell time and I bet you did. Oh yes, how is your school? Well, I have to teach at cooking school now as I have made mess sergeant. I think we will leave here in December. We have been told that so much that I don't know for sure just when we will go.

Well, Honey, I feel sort of low tonight. If I just had a nice letter from you maybe I would be okay. After I finish this I guess I will get out my old guitar for a little entertainment.

Honey, please write as often as you can for I miss your mail more than anything. For now, bye-bye.

Yours,
Red

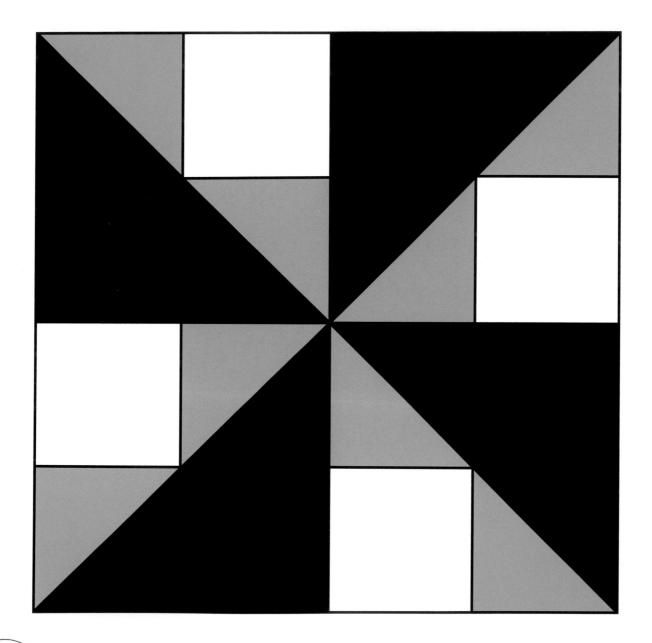

Carter O. Lilly and Genny N. Brun

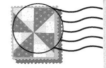

November 3, 1943

Our Date After the War

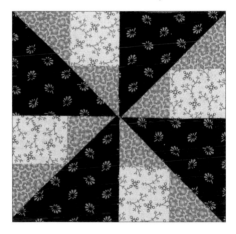

Dear Ginny,

I just got a sweet but short letter from you. But anyways, I was happy to get it. Today is Sunday and a very beautiful day here. Wish you were here now.

Yes, Honey, I realize it has been 14 months since we met, but 14 years won't cause me to forget the sweetest person I have ever known. I will remember our date after the war. I hope that the war doesn't keep us waiting too long. Say Honey, maybe I can find some shells here somewhere if you tell me what kind and size to get. I'll sure try. And don't forget the gun I promised you. I have a nice one now if I get to keep it.

Well, tomorrow I have to go to camp and go through an Army course with guns firing only 18 inches over us while we're crawling, so let's hope I can crawl yet like I did 25 years ago. Ha ha.

Ginny, it's awful sweet of you to want to be a nurse's aide, but I wish you wouldn't. It's bad for your nerves and all that. Does your big sis like that?

Oh, yes! Yesterday I had a swell time with the family that lives by our place here. My girl isn't as pretty as you, so it would have been better still if you could have been here. Well, Honey, I have to go to work, so please don't make me wait for a nice long letter from my very nicest best friend. Send me a snap of you, too. I have a new card case and I want a picture of you that will fit in it.

Bye Darling,
Red

Robert Paul DeWalt

Robert Paul DeWalt was born on July 30, 1918 in North Baltimore, Ohio. His family moved in the 1930s to Wyandotte, Michigan, where he enlisted in World War II in early 1942. He served in the U.S. Army Air Corps and was sent to New Guinea. Robert writes his letters home to his mother, Gladys DeWalt, often mentioning his sweetheart and future wife, Reba Marie Yates.

Reba was born on October 23, 1922 in Findlay, Ohio. She met Robert on a blind date before the war. When Robert was not writing letters home to his mother, he wrote letters home to Reba.

Robert and Reba were married on July 3, 1944. Together they had one child, a daughter they named Gladys after Robert's mother. Robert was a pipe fitter and master welder, and he worked at many of the factories in Detroit, Michigan that helped build energy plants. Robert passed away in 2003, with Reba passing shortly thereafter in 2006.

Coca-Cola Company-Issued Sewing Kit

Robert DeWalt with his father
Wallace and mother Gladys.

Robert and Reba (nee Yates) DeWalt
on their wedding day.

V-mail, or victory mail, were microfilmed
versions of full-size letters meant to save space
and time in delivery, especially overseas.
Photographed here is a collection of Robert's
V-mail letters.

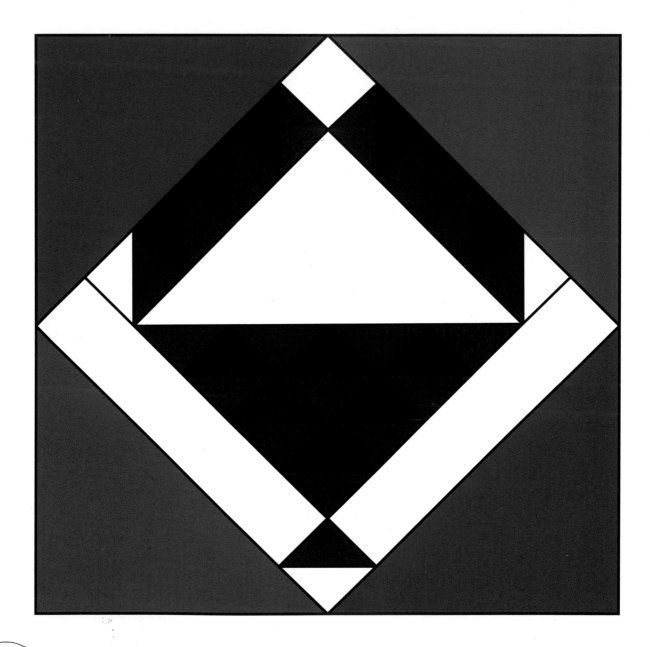

Robert Paul DeWalt

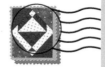

Technical School

February 7, 1941

Hello Mom and All,

I finally got a long train ride out of Uncle Sam anyway. They sent us out here in God's country. I'm sure only God would have it. All I have seen here is dust. Ha.

I can't tell you much about this place because I only got here this afternoon. They told us we would only be here about three weeks or a month. We have to drill seven days a week and we can't leave the camp, so don't worry about me getting into trouble. Ha.

I am still in the dark as to what they will do with me. I'm supposed to be in a technical school squadron, but I haven't seen anything technical about it yet. They might teach us to march here and then send us to school. I don't know for sure.

This place is about five miles from Wichita Falls, wherever that is. I don't expect to see it. On the way out here I made pretty good friends with a young German about my age. He only came from Germany about nine years ago. The odd thing is that he is a welder too, and his name is DeWall. Pretty close, eh?

I don't believe I have much more to say this time, Mom. After a few days I should have something worthwhile to say.

Love,
Bob

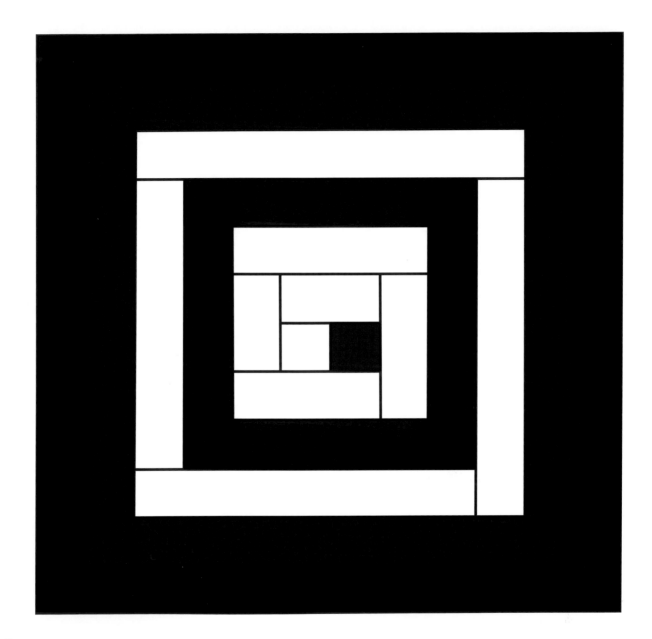

Robert Paul DeWalt

194

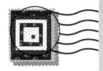

March 13, 1942

A Soldier's Dream

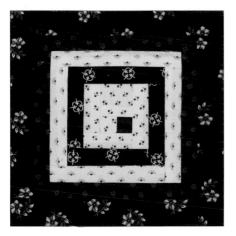

Hello Mom,

How is everything back home? I hope you all feel as well as me. These sea breezes really put the spring in my step. I suppose Francis is back to normal by this time? I wondered what it was. Has Reba written to you yet? I think she is about half afraid of you since you used to be a school teacher. I'm getting pretty lonesome for a letter from anybody, but I expect to wait at least another week if I am here that long.

It is dark now, I just came in from the outside. I was looking out across the bay at the lights from Oakland and San Francisco. It is a wonderful view, something a civilian can't see. I get a great satisfaction out of that anyways. Ha. I wish I could stay here. It wouldn't be hard to take at all. Mom, I can stand out there and just smell the flowers any time. Can you imagine an army camp like that?

The food here is like something from a soldier's dream that he seldom gets. They set the butter and milk out on the table and we sit down and help ourselves. We are really making up for Sheppard Field grub I didn't want to complain while I was there, but I can tell you now that it was pretty terrible. Not only the food, but the whole personnel. If the whole army were trained by officers so vague, it wouldn't be worth much.

I still don't know much about my future or where I am going. However, we are going to get rifles here, so it looks like we will be sent on guard duty. Most are pretty sore about it. A lot of us are mechanics and welders. If we have to go out here and stand by some bridge for the duration, it isn't going to go down so good. Every bridge and tunnel I saw in California has at least two men guarding it. You should see the planes around here. They are flying around all the time, and a big battle wagon sits in the mouth of the bay. It sure is comforting to see it.

I have it pretty nice here, Mom. I sleep in a semiprivate room with only three other fellows. The Sgt. and I are pretty close. He used to be my catcher back at Sheppard Field. Ha.

Much love to all,
Bob

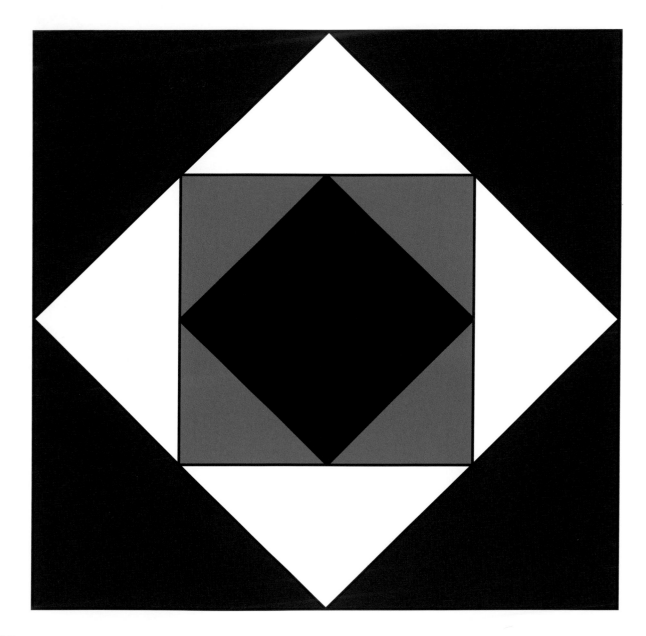

Robert Paul DeWalt

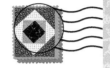

Land of the Way Down Under

April 19, 1942

Dear Mom and All,

I suppose you have been waiting a long time for word from me. I wanted to write but I just haven't had the chance. We were not allowed to write until the last couple of days. I believe the government has notified you as to where I am. I guess they call it the Land of the Way Down Under Australia. I know you realize how far that is, Mom. I hate to think of it myself. It seems rather futile to start a letter off on that distance.

I am still in the same department. Things go along as usual but I still haven't been given my line of work. I would feel a lot better if I had. There is a lot I would like to tell you, Mom, like where I am and what I do, but I can't because of censorship.

I like these Australians a lot and they seem to like us Yanks, too (especially the girls) I have been invited to private houses a number of times for tea. I really enjoy every occasion. I like to hear them talk. When I come home I will give you an imitation or two. Ha.

How is everything at home? I hope everyone is well. I suppose we have a new addition to our clan now. I hope he or she is doing well and also the mother. Sometimes I get pretty lonesome for you, Mom. That goes for Dad and all the rest, too. If I could hear from someone now and then, it wouldn't be so bad. I shouldn't complain, I have things pretty nice compared with a lot of people in this world. Do you ever hear from Reba? I hope so, because I want to keep her in the family. I have traveled a good way and seen a lot of girls, but not one could take her place.

Do you still buy a defense bond every two weeks? If everyone were as serious about this thing as you, I'm sure the war wouldn't last long. I still hope to be home in 10 months or a year. These Australians have their head set on a quick victory. I'm sure it will be that way. I guess I will have to close now. If I knew for sure what I could say, it wouldn't be so bad. Half of this might be blacked out when you get it.

Love to all,
Bob

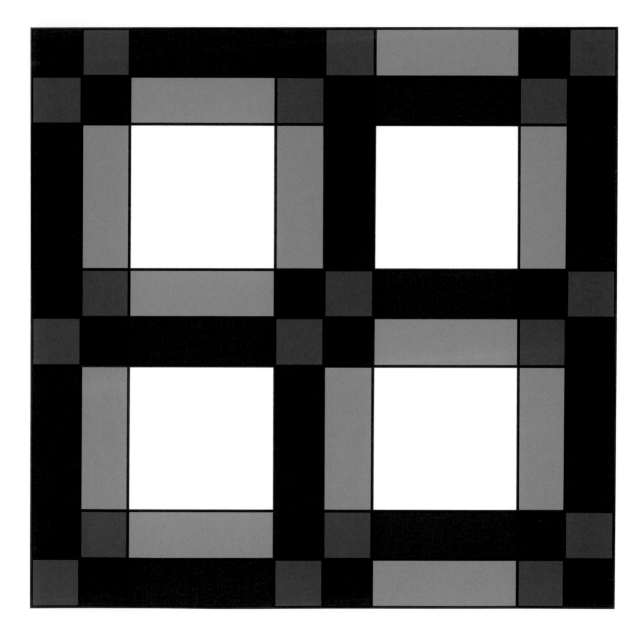

Robert Paul DeWalt

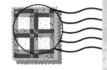

June 17, 1942

Yellow Jaundice

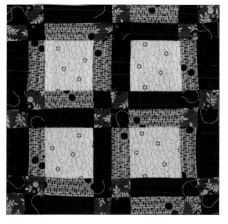

Hello Mom and All,

How is everyone at home? Very well, I hope. I suppose you and Dad have your garden out by now, don't you, Mom? I am still enjoying winter. It never snows here, but neither does it shine. I did enjoy a short summer when we crossed the equator. In fact, I had all I wanted of that imaginary line. Ha.

I was sorry to hear you say that Tommy had been taken into the service. I don't think he was built for this life. Has Emil managed to get in yet? I hope he gets in the air corps. The infantry would be pretty tough.

I have plenty of time to write these days. I am surviving my first hitch in a hospital. I have jaundice catarrhal, better known as yellow jaundice. I don't feel bad, but I have a hard time eating. I have been here three days. How much longer it will be, I don't know.

I suppose Rieny is as happy as a kid with a new toy since he is running an engine. I bet Jake has to look at his laurels nowadays. Ha. How is Durb getting along in his new home? Is he still on the wagon? Tell him I nearly had that grass skirt bagged for him, but there were a few too many sharks in between it and me. Ha.

I rather expected some mail today, but I didn't get any. It's been more than a month now since the last. I would write more, but the postal system is so poor, it seems useless. I got a letter from Reba. That was pretty good. I would like you to send me a package, Mom. Just put anything you can find in it. I'm not particular anymore. You might put some whipped cream in, too. Ha. I am waiting for those reduced prices on cablegrams. When we get them, you will hear from me more often.

Did it break Dad up much when Ginger passed away? I was sorry to hear it. He will have to train Jim to fetch now. Do you ever go down home, Mom? I am wondering if you ever saw Reba. I would like to see one of her letters to you. I just can't figure out what she would have to say. I will have to close now. It's time for my thermometer. Ha.

Love to all,
Bob

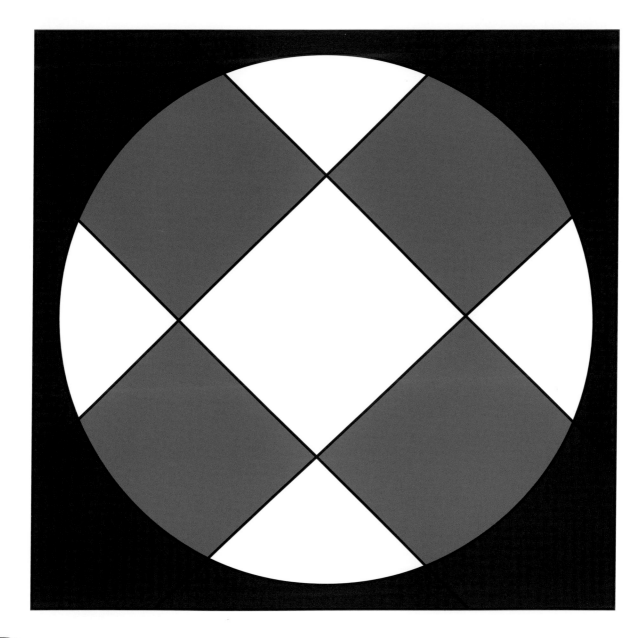

Robert Paul DeWalt

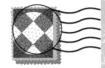

July 10, 1942

Hello Mom,

I received a letter from you last night. It was a good bit older than some I have gotten, but still a letter. I have been getting a lot more mail lately and it suits me fine. I got one from Reba, too, dated the same. I don't have a whole lot of time to write anymore. I go to work at 7:30 every morning and I don't get back till about 6:00. By the time I eat and get cleaned up, I only have about two hours in which to write. There is another party apart from you and Reba to whom I am obliged to write, also.

I am working at my line all the time now, Mom. I only use acetylene, though. I might get some stripes pretty soon if I can keep myself in line. I have my doubts about that, however. We haven't gotten leave for a long time, so I am about ready. I think the situation looks pretty good now. I know there will be some tough times yet, but I think we are nearly over the hump.

It is July now. I suppose the weather is well back there. It doesn't seem right to me, as you know what the season is south of the equator. I suppose you have read in the papers about how the boys are getting along with the girls here. It is pretty true. I know several fellows from my outfit that have taken wives here. It won't be so bad as long as they remember they're married after the peace comes. You need not worry about me though, I may as well wait longer so I can say I was a bachelor. I want you to throw a party on my birthday, Mom. I will not be there, but the rest of you can have a good time. I will be there in thoughts.

Love,
Bob

South of the Equator

Robert Paul DeWalt

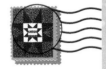

August 31, 1942

V-Mail and Packages

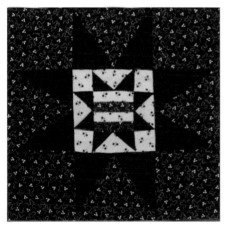

Dearest Mom,

I hope this finds you all well. I have been doing a lot of writing lately. I have been receiving a lot of mail in the last several weeks. I tried to answer it all. I not only have all of you back there, but several over here. I got a letter from you last night dated June 23. That was before you had heard from me, you mentioned Joe working seven days a week. How does he like it? I wish you could let me know just what he does.

What do you think of the V-mail? I suppose you have had some from me by this time. Reba doesn't like it so much. I haven't had any yet, but I imagine it is hard to get accustomed to. I received a package from Reba. Two cartons of smokes, a box of Whitman's chocolates, stationery and her picture. The picture is perfect. I was never so glad to get anything. I made a special shelf above my bunk for it.

She told me you received my snapshot. I'm sure you found me just the same, which I am. Reba complimented me on the nice looking girl. I'm sorry I forgot to tell you she is a man's wife. I rushed a V-mail off to her to put things straight. Hot. Did she have a good time up at our place? She said she did.

Tomorrow is my day off, Mom. I think I will go to town and try to buy up a supply of film. It is getting scarce here. Today was my payday, so I might even bend my elbow a few times. Don't worry, Mom, I can still resist. I drew 16 pounds and 10 shillings. Would you like to figure it out, Mom? Ha. $53.74.

Love,
Bob

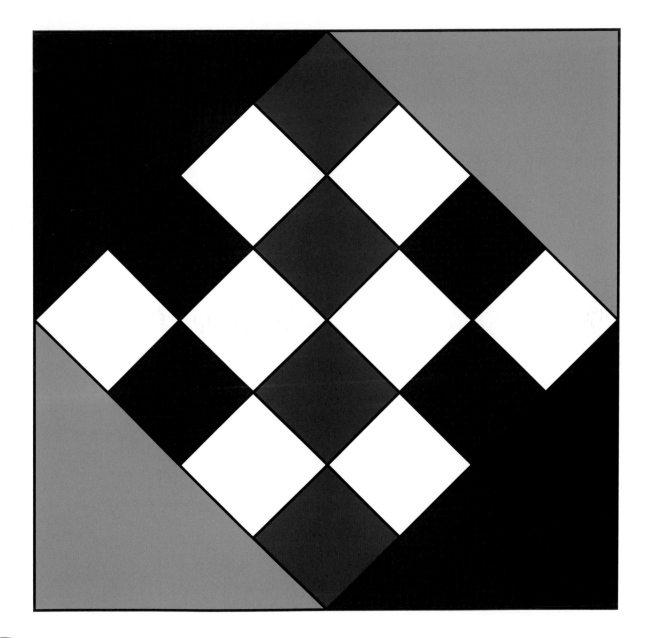

Robert Paul DeWalt

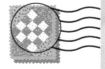

April 26, 1943

Dearest Mom and All,

I trust this will find you all in the very best of health. Are you still a working girl, Mom? You and that job together give me quite a kick at times. You seem to be in quite a rush these days, always dashing off a letter before going to work. Ha. As for me, I am feeling fine physically but not in mind. I should be quite content. I received letters from you, and Francis and Mary both yesterday, and today, a very delicious cake from Betty, but not from Reba for it seems ages.

You can imagine my state of mind. This old dog face is really quite perturbed. Could it be that my conduct in Australia has drifted halfway around the world? Mom, you didn't by chance make a slip, did you? I have been writing to her several times a week lately. Perhaps she has begun to take me for granted. If so, I can soon put a different complexion on the picture. I'll have you show her a few of those snapshots. Ha ha. I'm sending you those snaps again after removing the locations. If I had never been in this part of the world, I probably wouldn't have thought of giving you a picture like the one of the natives, but after living among these people, such things become commonplace and we think nothing of it. After being here a short while one can easily understand the lack of clothing. Since I have been going without a shirt, it is twice as uncomfortable when I do wear one.

I see Father Dickerson died. That's too bad when a man goes through life never knowing what treasures it held for him. I'll call a halt to this morning. I just can't strike a happy medium tonight. I'm trying to be jolly to cover up my breaking heart. It won't work. Ha. I wish Dad would throttle you down a bit. I think you are burning up too much petrol these days. Good night, Mom.

Love,
Bob

A Few
Snapshots

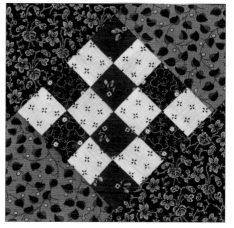

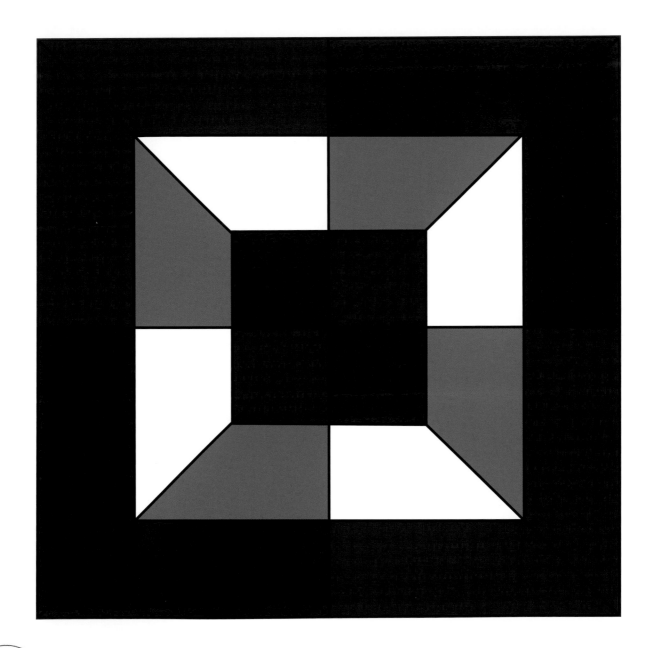

Robert Paul DeWalt

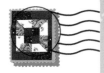

September 26, 1943

Dear Mom,

Have been sitting here trying to decide to whom I would write — you or Reba — as there is only time for one letter. Well, I guess I love my Mom more than anyone tonight, so to you, my dear, it is. Glad you're back to normal after that spell. I understand that the male of the species is usually more fragile physically, but Dad seems to be the one with the iron constitution in our abode. Ha!

By the way, I got a package from you yesterday and also a letter for September 6. The chocolates were in a pretty bad way, but despite the mildew I really liked them. It is pretty warm here now, so things just can't help but melt. It seems foolish to call it summer, it's just hotter than usual.

I have taken up one roll of film so far. They seem to be all right but don't send any more for several months. I don't have much time these days for sightseeing. Only a day a week. Besides, you all must be getting tired of my face. I might get a three-day leave soon to do some seeing and snapping.

I also want to negotiate for transfer. I have no complaints about this outfit, just want to get back to 503. I do my own line of work here and get along okay but this thing of starting all over again to get acquainted is getting old with me. There are four sergeants in our shop and me. Frightfully jolly, eh? I can safely say I don't forget more than a couple of them now, but that cuts no ice. You know my disposition, Mom. That must be the bottleneck.

Thanks for sending Reba a birthday gift. I made her a ring from a shilling. I might save money on it, too, if I can get her to use that for a wedding ring. Ha. Got a letter from Francis with some good snaps. She seems to have changed more than anyone. Since her first letter to me she has developed into a very entertaining correspondent. It seems that she is doomed to become a bookworm. No doubt to get her out of work in later years and a good idea. Ha.

Well, Mom, Pop and all, this, as you say, seems to be the lot. You shouldn't wish certain people into the Army. They may be stationed in Australia. There is nothing grim or unpleasant in that deal. Ha. Cheerio.

Love,
Bob

Negotiate for Transfer

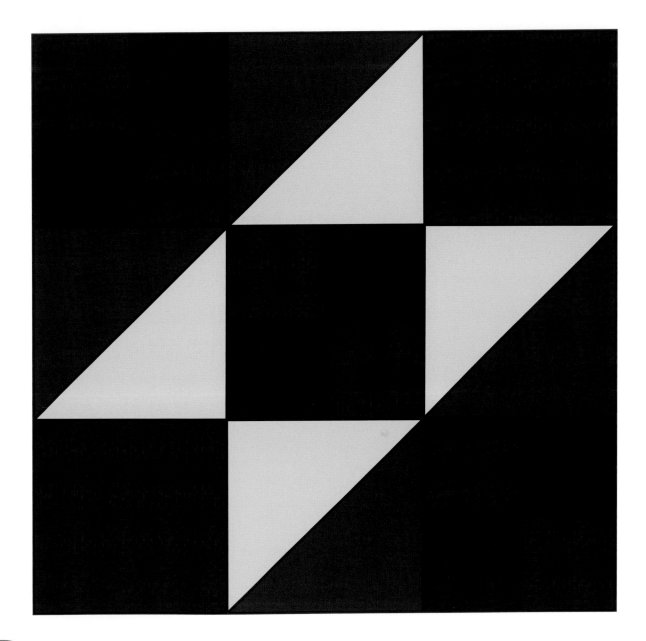

Robert Paul DeWalt

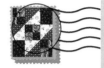

October 4, 1943

Dear Mom and All,

I started to write you this afternoon, but gave up in disgust as there was nothing of importance to report on. Well, it's a marvel how a few hours can change the whole perspective of one's outlook. I'm bursting with chatter, as one of the boys came up a while ago with the parcel letters for me. It had been more than a week since hearing from you. It's sure good to hear from home and to know that everyone is well. There were pictures from Francis of the kids. That one of Davie kissing Paul is sure a prizewinner. The boys around here know all those kids by now and think they are nuts. Some day those kids will be surprised when I tell them how popular they were down in the South West Pacific.

Well, Mom, did Davie say how he liked KP? I bet he loved it like I did. If it's like it was when I was there, well, there's no letup for about 16 hours. I have been pretty lucky about keeping away from it down here, always managed to have something on this string to get me out of it. The secret is to get a job that no one else can handle or doesn't want to. Ha.

I don't think there are really any rules or regulations in regard to the length of service overseas. In peacetime a soldier knows where he stands, but this is war, so I need to say more. I think Reba is going on the supposition of that old 18 month rerun. I just can't be so brutal as to tell her what I really think.

Glad you got the letter from Betty. She isn't much of a letter writer, but despite that fall, she is still the nicest gal I have met in Aussie. I asked her to write you once and tell you about my vacation. I expected to be dropped after that. She and I just met and had a good time together for two days, and thus parted. That's the end of it. I'm taking no more outside correspondence, although I can't say I would like to. Ha.

You know Mom, I'm not quite like the boy who used to sit nights and read with you. I really busted loose in Australia. I didn't change my ideas in any important ways, but I think I'll be a better mixer after I get home. I think some people used to think me a snob. They had the wrong idea, but I didn't care. But that's not the way to look at it, I guess. Well Mom, this seems about it, so cheerio till next time.

Love,
Bob

Rules or Regulations

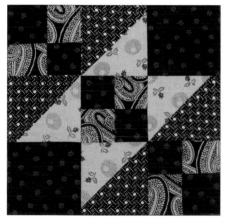

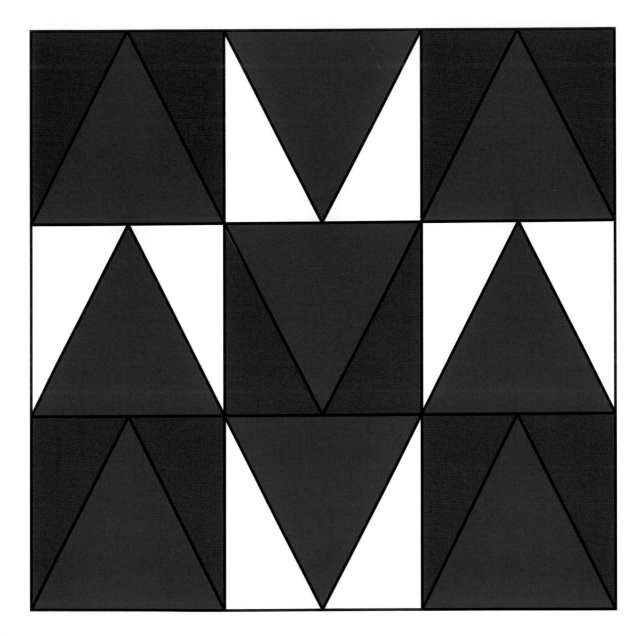

Robert Paul DeWalt

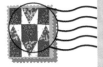

November 11, 1943

Let Down My Sweethearts

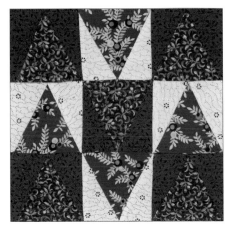

Dear Mom and All,

I received all kinds of letters yesterday. I was elated. Two each from my three Old Faithfuls, also one from Grandma. Glad to hear Reba was up. She told me about her good time. She informed me that you gave away our bed. Ha! What's all this about making table talk? I've been hearing about some of its predictions for quite a while now but didn't think much of it. Now, Mom, you state it has even you guessing. I have begun to wonder. As for me being home by Christmas, why I'm afraid someone is way off. As much as I would like to be, I can't see it. It will grieve me something terrible to let down my sweethearts. Ha. Seriously though, I don't think I'll be back before too awful long. They will have to fetch us back before we become aliens.

I have had a streak of bad luck here of late. Remember I said Muriel was away when I got back here? No sooner than she got back when off she went to the hospital with an attack of appendicitis. All I got out of it was a short phone conversation. Perhaps it was just as well? Then yesterday, while Christmas shopping, I was doing just fine when I fell down and busted open my lower lip which took about four stitches. When I get back at least I'll look like an old war hoss anyway. The boys tell me I'm also getting a little bit bald in the back. Guess I'm lucky to have such a good prospect for a wife while I am still half presentable.

Don't know if I'm glad or not to hear about Francis and another blessed event. My laundry lady gives me reason for such thinking. She is only about 30 and already has eight children. I shudder to think of my folks going to such extremes. I have definite plans made on that matter. Wouldn't mention them though, because I will probably get the how when they go on the rocks.

Here it is, Mom. I have to get to work. PMs this week. I want you to write and tell me all about how you found Reba to be. Cheerio all.

Love,
Bob

Robert Paul DeWalt

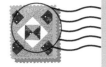

December 31, 1943

Mom,

Well, here it is New Year's Eve again. I wonder what all of you folks will be doing tonight. I bet my Mom and Pop are staying sober anyway. That's a pleasant thought, as I only had two beers today. I went to town and got two-months pay this afternoon. I'm off on a furlough tomorrow. I am anxious to see the old friends, especially Bill and Marge. Haven't decided yet whether or not to call Betty. You hadn't told me about her being sick. I suspect I should call out of courtesy, eh, Mom? Ha.

Don't know for sure yet if I'll get to go to the place I mentioned before. I only have one roll of film, so I probably won't if I can't find more. I don't have much desire to see a place unless I can get it down on film for you all to enjoy. Of course, I also imagine people won't believe me about the spots I have been in unless I have the snaps to prove it. Ha.

Haven't heard from Don for some time. I know he is at college but not where. I understand some mail and a good many packages were recently lost, so that is some I won't get. Sent several calendars to you, Mom. Take the one you like and give the others to the girls. I sent you some literature recently on Australian flowers. The book set me back one guinea so you better enjoy it. Ha!

I had a good time last night. Went with Muriel and her sister Eileen to visit a Mr. and Mrs. Smith. They live on the very top of a high hill overlooking town. It is one of a few cool spots in this vicinity. Well, Muriel and Mrs. Smith played the fiddle and Eileen the piano. Eileen is a very good singer and very pretty gal. Her husband has been a prisoner for nearly two years. She has had two cards from him so far. Ain't that something.

Well, I had a jolly good time. It is an Aussie custom at such get-togethers for everybody to solo at least one song. Well, I got up and gave them "Waltzing Matilda" in my ripping baritone. You can't imagine me being so bold, now can you? Perhaps it's my old age creeping up. The old man, Mr. Smith, gave me a tip on a horse. I won $13, so I intend to partake of more such evenings. Will write to you from the country beyond. Cheerio.

Love to all,
Bob

New Year's Eve Again

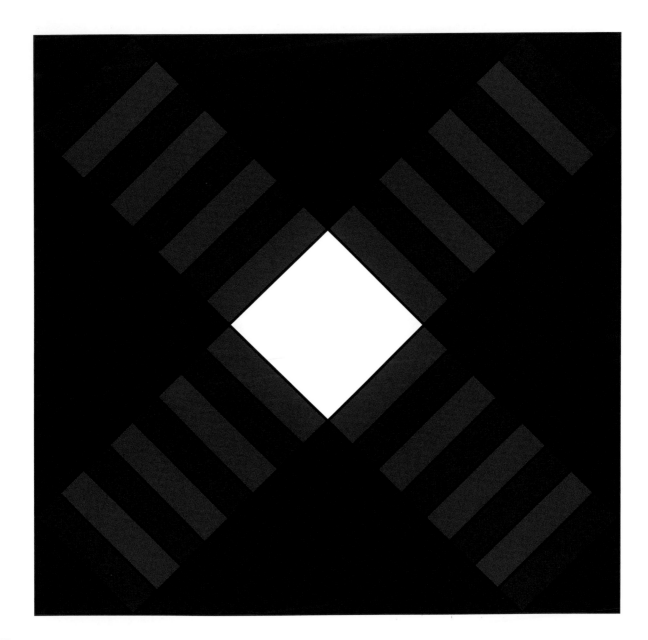

Robert Paul DeWalt

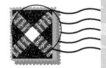

February 7, 1944

Here in Sunny Virginia

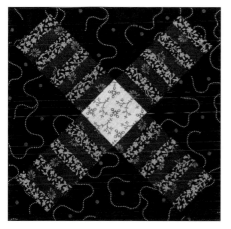

Hello Folks,

How's everybody? The best, I hope. We are doing fine. But believe it or not, it's pretty hard at times to keep warm down here in sunny Virginia. They don't supply much heat at night, but then they are right in figuring we can keep warm somehow.

Mom, were you planning a chicken dinner for me this Sunday? Well, I want you all to enjoy it and eat an extra piece for me as I won't be able to make it. The fellow who filled out my furlough request form got it all balled up (or maybe I told him wrong). Anyhow, it was approved for March 10th instead of February 10th. I am trying to get it changed, but I will probably be delayed a week or so.

Incidentally, I reckon it's about time to divulge the fact that I'm going to be a father. Reba went out to the hospital today. The doctor said the new member will spring in mid-August. I'm trying to decide whether Reba should stay home. As for her, well, I'm just learning how "easy" it is to get along with a pregnant woman!

(This part of the letter was written by Reba) And if the expectant mother is so easy to get along with, you should see the papa to be. He is nearly as bad as an old mother hen. He thinks he is going to send me home to stay, but for the present, at least, my feet are planted on solid ground here in Virginia. There are four of the girls in our crowd expecting and if they can stay, I think I can. Won't you tell your son babies are being born every day and his will be no different than the rest? He may listen to you and keep me here. We are both pretty happy in spite of all our talk, so don't pay too much attention to our goings on. Cheerio all.

Love,
Bob and Reba

Robert Paul DeWalt

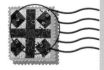

May 19, 1944

Dear Mom and All,

Whopping Big T-Bone Steak

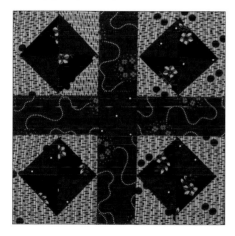

Got a letter from you today, postmarked the 11th. That is a new record for me. The boys in California usually get their mail about two days quicker than I. No kidding, Mom, you write the most interesting letters. So much news and so few words. Wish I had the knack. Reba's mother wrote to me recently, she told me more about the family and hometown affairs in that one letter than Reba has in two years, but I suppose it takes a few years to get the nonsense out of one's head. Ha.

I just came in from town. I had one whopping big T-bone steak. Such wonderful things don't happen to me often, so I consider it well worth writing about. There is quite a milk shortage at present. The powdered variety is plentiful in camp but it ain't for me. The only way we can have eggs is to be lucky enough to dream of them. Excuse me, Mom, I forgot that you probably read all this in your Sunday paper.

Well, the long-awaited Wacs got here in force recently. They are the toast of the town at present. You should see these Aussie girls give them the once over. It tickles me pink. These gals have come to reckon they are the cream of the earth. Before we came here, there were about a dozen women to one man. It is just that about now. Consequently, they have changed from the clinging vine approach to the cold shoulder. Maybe the war will put them back on their beam. Ha.

You might think I talk like I've been jilted, well, a few times but not enough to make me bitter. I'm just disgusted with this mess. If I weren't coming home, I'd make tracks for the islands and dig in until it's over. The squadron is throwing a party tomorrow, might have 100 or so Wacs here. What a comedy of wolf eat wolf that will be. Ha. Cheerio all.

Love,
Bob

P.S. Mom, if Reba comes up give her a kiss for me. Swear I'll never mention dates again.

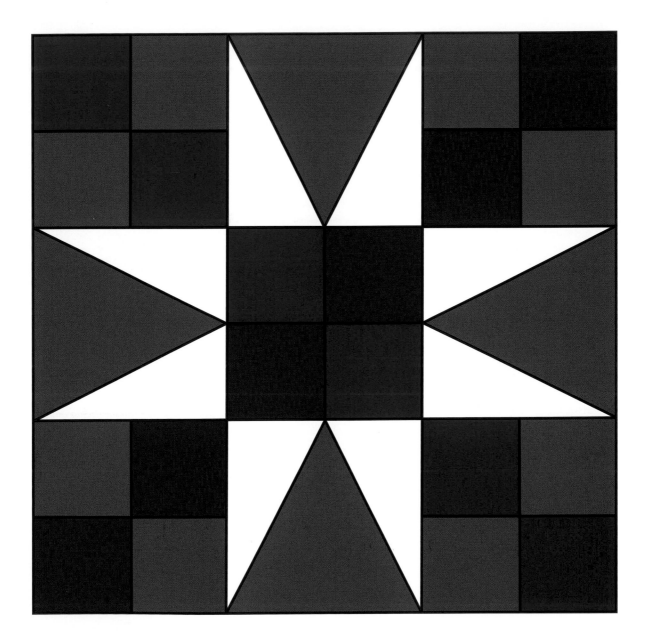

Robert Paul DeWalt

218

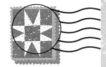

July 28, 1944

No Chance of a Discharge

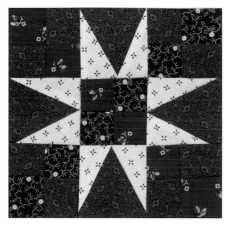

Dear Mom, Dad and All,

Well here I am, arrived Wednesday morning at eight o'clock in Miami Beach. Should have written sooner but have been too busy trying to find a cool spot. I'm not doing much here but loafing while I'm not in processing. What I mean by that is interviews, examinations and so on. Had a complete physical today. Sorry to say there is no chance of a discharge as they found me in a quite robust condition. Have gained exactly 15 pounds since joining.

Well, there isn't much I can say about this place, as my young brother before me probably gave a better description than I could ever, but it is a bit of all right. This room I have here would cost a tourist 25 or 30 bucks per week. It overlooks the swimming pool, which is in the patio of this U-shaped building. The ocean is only a few yards beyond. There is a nice breeze, which is all right at night, but the days are too hot for any breeze to cool. Did Davie complain of the heat when he was here? If not, he must be a better man than I.

If I could slop around without a shirt it would be all right, but they must be worn at all times (excepting the beach). And ties after six o'clock? That kills me. I telegrammed Reba tonight and asked her to come down. If she does I will have to be very sweet, because this climate sure won't make her happy. There are so many things to do here, but I don't feel like moving without that gal around. However, I might go deep sea fishing tomorrow. It's all free. Reba has never seen a place like this, it will tickle me to watch her gape in awe.

Well, Mom, this seems to be it. There is still one to go to my wife. She takes up a lot of time in writing and thinking. Ha. Cheerio all.

Love,
Bob

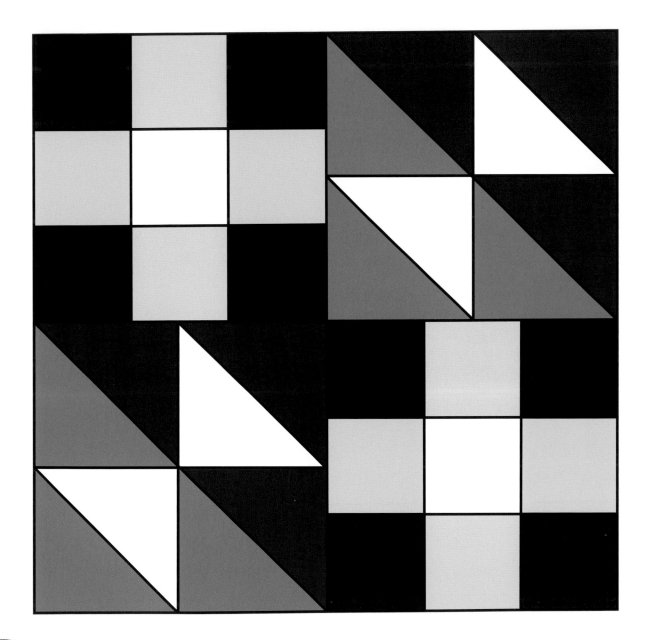

Robert Paul DeWalt

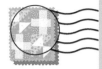

B-29 Training Base

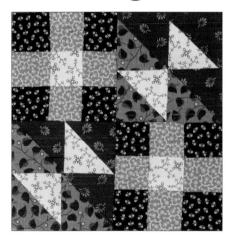

August 30, 1944

Dear Mom and All,

How's everyone these days? If it is as cold there as here in Geneva, Nebraska, you must be in your furs. I am okay, but so tired of traveling. However, I may get to catch my breath here for a few months. Got off the train at Fairmont last night. There's about half a dozen houses and a general store. It looks like a tough proposition for Reba out here. Omaha seems to be the only town larger than a hamlet in the vicinity, and it's too far.

I start work in the shop tomorrow night. Haven't got the lay of the place yet, so we'll have details later. It's a B-29 training base, the address stands for overseas training unit, very heavy, Fairmont Army Airfield. Mom, will you send my uniforms? We have to start wearing them September 10th. They will put the screws to me if I don't have them.

Well, I have to close, Mom. I want to catch a bus at five for the town of York where the USO might help me in finding a place. There is a heavy bomb group here at present, which should leave in a few weeks. They should leave some vacancies.

Mom, I haven't heard from you in ages. How about that? Cheerio all.

Love,
Bob

Robert Paul DeWalt

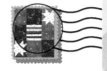

November 25, 1944

Dear Mom and Dad,

How's everybody these days? Haven't heard for some time so how about shaking a pen, Mom? I haven't been so hot at it either but, well, that's different. I'm busy. Hot. I'm in charge of quarters tonight, so I might find time to write to the best of my ability for a change.

Reba and I planned to make this quite a Thanksgiving till this came up. But I'll try to make the best of it in catching up on my writing. We had a good supper. Turkey and all the trimmings. There is a party and dance going on in the mess hall now. It's up to me to keep peace among the GIs and Wacs. Free beer which I can't touch. That's awful.

Well, we haven't moved yet. They sprayed the place well, so we haven't found any bugs lately. That's helped Reba a lot. That girl is really spooked, you know.

Quite a Thanksgiving

How is brother Don doing these days? Is he keeping up the subjects only with social life? Let me know when he expects to go home next so I can arrange a furlough for then. I want to see the lad very much. I am sorry Francis and Rieny can't make it down here, but I am expecting them in the spring.

It's not too cold here but the river gives off some cold breezes. I'm anxious to see the first snow, which I hear there is very little here. Mom, you can send me a car for Christmas. We are getting tired of the city life here in Washington DC, riding trams and buses.

Will stop now and go make my rounds. The Wacs will probably give us trouble tonight! Hope you had an enjoyable Thanksgiving.

Much love,
Bob

P.S. I think Reba got the pictures today.

Robert Paul DeWalt

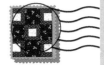

The Latest News

August 2, 1945

Dear Mom and All,

How are you feeling? The best I hope. Glad to hear that Aleva is doing well. Diana suits me all right. I suppose Don knows by now if he is going to be a brass hat or not. I hope so. I may get to see him yet.

Has Reba told you the latest news? The baby will be another week or so on the hatch. What little fortitude I had is fast ebbing. That old doctor of hers seems to be giving us the baby trot or something. I can't figure why he told her July 13th. Think I'll handle the next case personally.

It's perfectly all right, Mom, you not sending a birthday card to me. I prefer not to be reminded anymore. When is Dad's birthday? Francis and Don are the only exact dates I can remember. Ha. When is Mary coming out east? Soon, I'll take it. She might drop by my place to say hello. I can promise her a good steak dinner at our club.

Well, I suppose you two will be seeing some World Series games this fall. Yes, I have to admit my doubts of the Mets catching up. They are pretty good, but poorly managed in my opinion. If this Army would wake up and realize it is overstaffed by millions, I might be there with you all. Cheerio Mom and Dad.

Love,
Bob

Stephen C. Dvorak

Stephen C. Dvorak was born on January 15, 1922 in Bronx, New York. He attended Townsend Harris High School and later graduated from the Webb Institute with a degree in naval architecture and marine engineering.

While still a student at the Webb Institute, Stephen left school and enlisted in the United States Army, serving as a technician during World War II. He wrote his letters home to his mother. She was more than happy to maintain a correspondence with her son, sending motherly advice, expressing her love, and telling him how much his letters meant to her.

After the war, Stephen returned to the Webb Institute to finish school. He later attended Columbia University and received a master's degree in mechanical engineering. He continued his career in marine engineering, working for different shipyards and shipbuilding corporations. Stephen passed away in June of 2011 at the age of 89.

Decorative Envelopes
Decorative envelopes, or covers as some called them, were used during World War II to show patriotism and solidarity.

Stephen C. Dvorak

Mrs. Dvorak's collection of letters to Stephen, along with many of the newspaper clippings, church bulletins, and even a map from her excursion down the Hudson River that she enclosed in her letters.

Postcards Stephen received from his mother during the war.

Stephen posing with his mother in 1943.

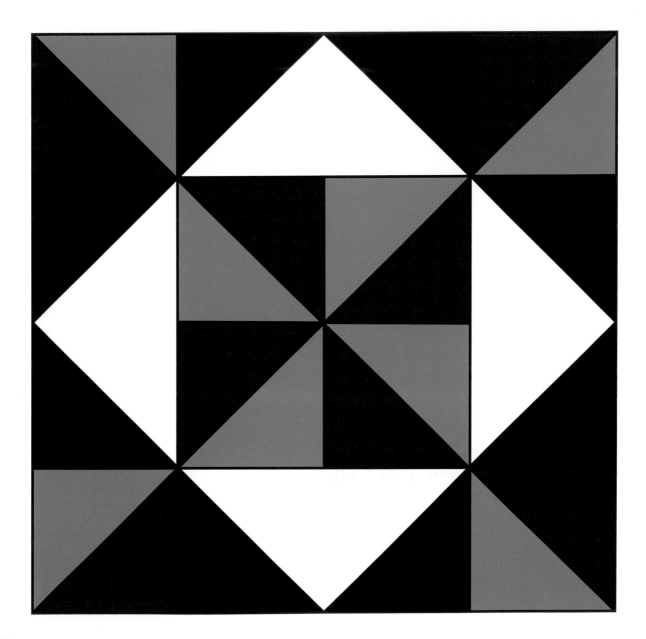

228

Stephen C. Dvorak

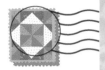

Memory Book of Yesterday

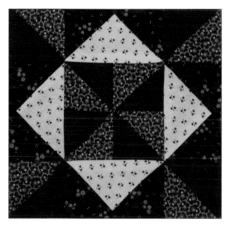

January 10, 1944

My Dear Son,

In my last letter I mentioned how I enjoyed the Christmas weekend. I did not have a Christmas tree this year. How happy I was to know that you had a grand Christmas weekend and so many lovely gifts from strangers.

Speaking of this morning, it is a very cold day and a real blizzard. It seems to me that something happened to my mind because lately I have forgotten to say Happy New Year to everyone. I started this letter on Sunday night. Today is Wednesday, and I am trying to finish it tonight.

I sent you a box of candy, I hope you enjoyed them. I am enclosing five dollars for your birthday also. Buy yourself something really nice. Though the day be gone, I want you to know I remembered your birthday.

Well, I wish you lots of good luck and happiness on your birthday. But when night comes, I can open the memory book of yesterday and dream dreams about you. Take care of yourself. Write soon. God bless you.

With Lots of Love to You,
Mother

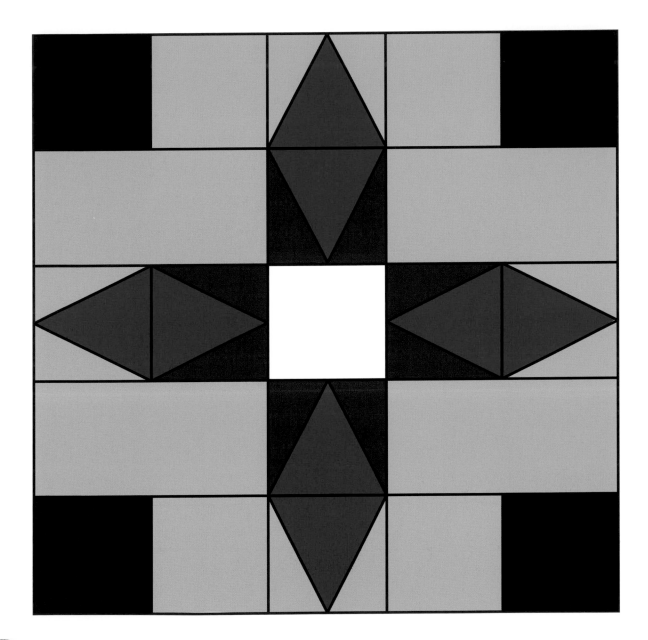

Stephen C. Dvorak

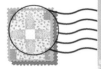

June 9, 1944

Going My Way

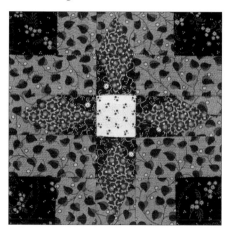

Dear Son,

It looks like we will have a nice cool day today. How are you feeling, all right? Another week has rolled by slowly. I received your letters and was disappointed to read that you didn't mention the $10 I sent you on May 29th. Let me know if you received it. Of course, it might have come after you sent the letter.

I received your package yesterday and you mentioned if I want to read your letters I can. I should like to say that as far as your letters go, I just couldn't read this week. I have been quite busy.

And so at last we have come to D-day, or rather the news of it reached us over the radio in the early hours of this morning. This makes me very, very sick, and I can't help it.

Last Sunday I went visiting to see Lizzie. She is well and sends you her best regards. Tuesday, I saw a good movie and it was very interesting. It was called *Going My Way*. Bing Crosby played the leading role. The story was about a young pastor who was trying to save his church from being mortgaged. It was a really nice picture and I enjoyed it very much.

Take care of yourself. I know I must close, let me hear from you soon. I do love you very much.

My Love and Blessings,
Mother

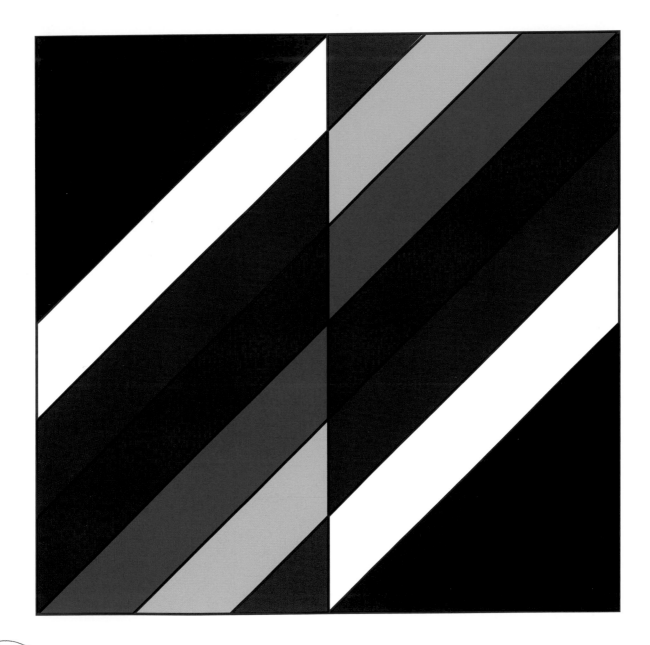

Stephen C. Dvorak

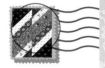

Brought Back Memories

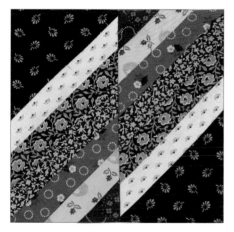

June 18, 1944

Dear Son,

I'm glad you're feeling good. I am feeling fine also. It has been very warm in New York, during the day and in the evenings. I spent a very interesting hour reading your letter about the lovely time you had at the young people's club meeting. I was glad to know that you are meeting all the lovely girls, too.

I hope you will get the money that I sent on time, and the cookies, too. Before I go any farther and say to return the money, when you have it to spare, I want you to use the money to buy a war bond. That will be a good savings for you.

Last Sunday I went to church service and it was children's day. It brought back memories of you, and it was the first time that I cried in a church service. I just can't help it. Many things happen, and sometimes I wonder if it is worthwhile to live.

I am thinking of your furlough and I hope you get it in August. When I received your letter, I was disappointed to read that you will be in school for a long time. Yes, in school is the best place to be these days, so as long as you are in school, I will have to be satisfied.

I look forward very much to the time when you are home again. Write soon. Take good care of yourself. God bless you.

All My Love,
Mother

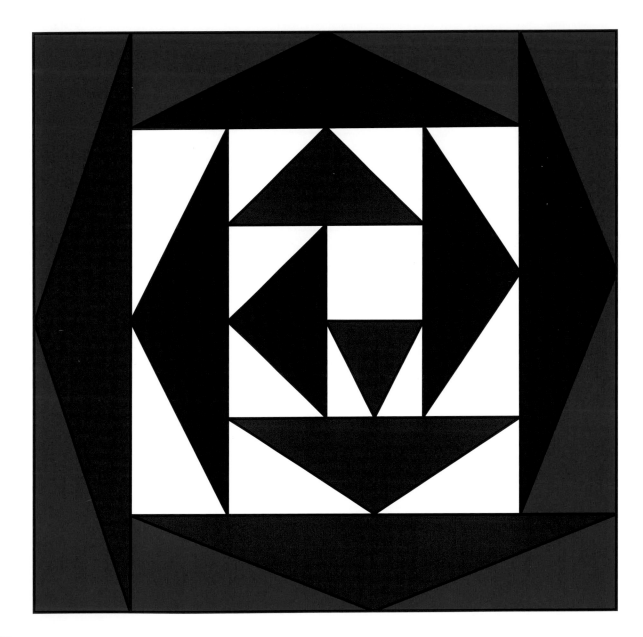

Stephen C. Dvorak

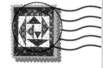

July 9, 1944

Hartford Circus Fire

Dear Son,

It is very, very hot in the city today. How about Camp Crowder? You should be glad to be away in the country some days—it would not be so much fun for you in a hot, smelly camp. Just get yourself up in the morning and breathe that fresh air.

I want you to have a good time and enjoy yourself while you can in this world. Last week I received a bond from the War Department. The summer sure goes by quickly, and soon it will be over.

I know that you read the *New York Times*. Did you read the bad news last week that the Hartford Circus fire killed 135? Many were trapped as L and N trains carrying troops fell into the river. It was very sad news.

You mentioned in your letter last time that I should try to go up the Hudson. Well, I tried on Wednesday, but it is so hard to go on a trip these days because everywhere you go there is a crowd of people. The boat was overcrowded and it didn't stop. Next time I try to go down the Hudson, I might have better luck.

Tuesday at dinnertime I had apple pie, country fried chicken and a wish you were here to help me finish up the chicken and pie. Every Sunday I'm cooking a big dinner like I used to, dreaming maybe you will surprise me and come home. Well, maybe my dream will come true, you never can tell.

On Monday I'm going to see *Snow White*, now playing in the Coliseum. I am glad that you are happy. How have you been? Write soon. God bless you.

All My Love,
Mother

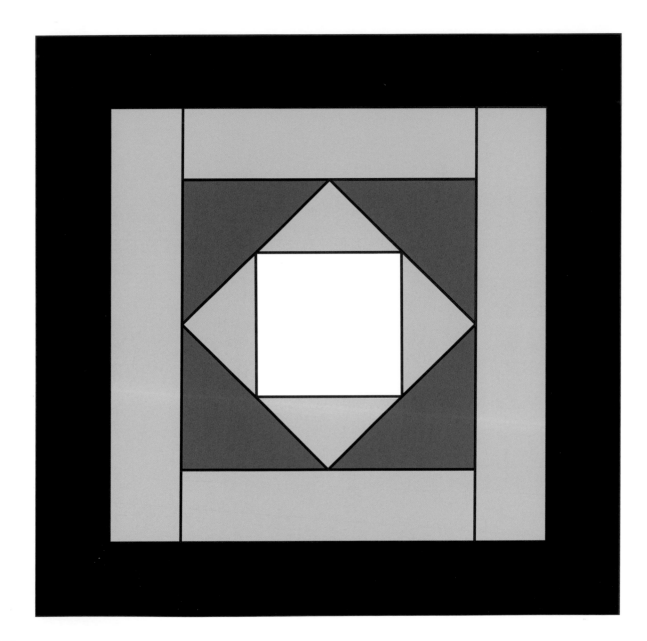

Stephen C. Dvorak

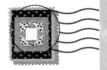

July 21, 1944

Sailed up the Hudson

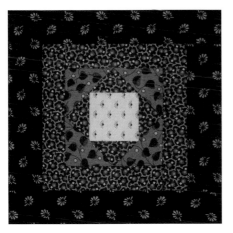

Dear Son,

How are you today? Almost a week ago I received your letter. Each hour this week sure flew by. As quickly as I looked around, it was already Thursday. Today I have time to write, so I will do it now.

I miss you very much, and I miss your very nice letters. Every time I receive a letter from you, I read it with great interest. I have never enjoyed anything as much as reading the letters that you send.

My little boy, I want you to have a good time. Do not worry about what Anna said. You study six days, you should have one day of rest.

Last Friday I sailed up the Hudson. The weather was really nice and I enjoyed myself.

Do you remember the nice time that we had three years ago? We were going to go places, those happy days. Write me again, and this time don't be so easy. Tell me if you liked the peach cakes I sent to you about two months ago. Don't forget to let me know.

I am very sorry I have not been able to write to you sooner. Right now it is late and you're probably sound asleep. I hope your dreams are very pleasant. Everything at home is just the same as always.

Write to me soon and be a good boy. God bless you with lots of love to you.

From,
Your Devoted Mother

Stephen C. Dvorak

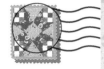

Both Pictures

July 28, 1944

Hello Sweetheart,

I hope that everything is all right with you today. I spent a very interesting hour reading your letters. In one letter you wrote about trouble again with your ingrown toenail. Please take care of your toe because you know your mother worries about you horribly.

Sunday it was wonderful to get up the Hudson again. This time I went with your brother Henry and his wife. The day was beautiful and warm and I enjoyed myself.

I hope the next trip up the Hudson we will all be together. You wanted to know why the boat was crowded. It's because, today, people can't get as much gasoline as they used to get before the war.

I have a very bad cold and a headache, but I've been having a good time here with movies. I saw a good movie on Monday called *Christmas Holiday*, and Wednesday I saw *The White Cliffs of Dover*. Both pictures were about love. I was very much pleased with both.

I kept thinking the other day what I would want to do when the war is over and you come home. Today I don't feel like I want to do a thing, I am taking a vacation. Nothing much is new at all.

Write soon and take good care of yourself. God bless you.

Lovingly Yours,
Mother

Stephen C. Dvorak

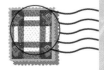

Sending the Cookies

August 3, 1944

Dear Son,

I received your letter and I am very glad that you are feeling good. I have been quite busy lately. On Sunday at dinner I had your friends Elliott and Madeline over. The dinner, I think, was good. I think you kind of like roast chicken and apple pie. All day Sunday I was hoping you'd come home. I can't help it; when Sunday comes, I miss you very much.

Tuesday night Anna and I were treated to a pair of tickets to see the new picture *Wilson*, which just opened at the movies. That was swell. Enclosed, you'll find a story about the picture.

Let me thank you for the pictures you sent. Please let me know when I should send the cookies. I received a letter from your friend, Lewis Hutton. I got an invitation to church, where he will be preaching on Sunday morning.

What are you doing with yourself? How are the girlfriends treating you? Write soon. Take care of yourself and have a good time. God bless you.

Love and Kisses From,
Your Mother

Stephen C. Dvorak

242

When the War Is Over

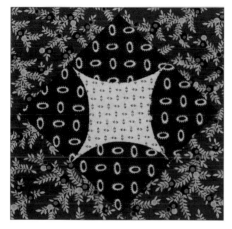

August 19, 1944

Dear Son,

I hope that everything is all right with you today. It is Saturday night here again. Today was a nice day, the sky was clear, and the wind was blowing cold all day. I spent the day on a roof watching the trains pass by and dreaming that I could get on the train and see you. Well, it was only a dream.

My last letter I made some mistakes writing about the two films. If you read last week's newspaper, you know the story of the pictures that I saw, Wilson and Heavenly Days.

You must learn to do as you are told to do, remember you are in the Army. You can go on a date with a beautiful blonde many times when the war is over. Tell me why you have to do so much training with so many weapons. The radio played this week. One week it is swell, then the next week bad.

Helen's birthday is August 28th. I received a letter from her, and I also received an invitation to go this weekend, only this week I don't feel so good to go. Next week I will try to go. Helen would like to hear from you very much. She said you didn't answer her letter.

Take care of yourself. God bless you. Good night, sleep tight and pleasant dreams.

Love,
Mother

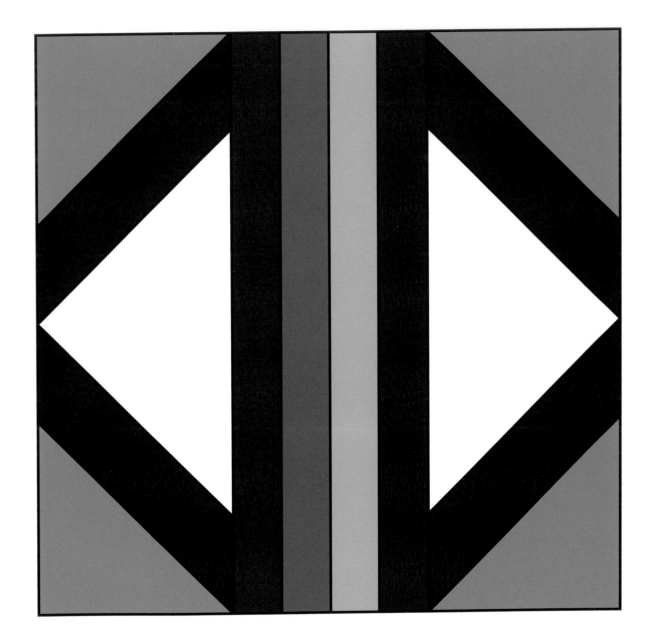

Stephen C. Dvorak

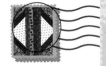

September 17, 1944

Your Love Affairs

Dear Son,

Perhaps you have been wondering why I haven't written to you for one week. You know, sometimes I just can't help it. I have no time to write to you. Each day there is so much to do or I might get fired. Anyway, thank you so much for your letter.

I think of you often and I am very happy to know you are coming home at the end of the year. It makes each hour of waiting a moment closer to the time when we shall be together again. I'm very happy to have your girlfriend Anna and look forward to seeing her soon.

Last week we had a horrible hurricane, and it was raining so hard the rain was coming through the windows. I was wishing that you were home that horrible night. I guess you know about the storm.

I am writing this letter to tell you that I want you to have a good time, Sweetheart. I'm not taking talk about your love affairs too seriously. Only just promise when the war is over, you will go back to Webb Institute. I know you are studying hard and I hope you do your very best, as hard as you can.

I hope you are feeling fine today. Twice I've asked you when I should send the cookies. Please give me an answer to my questions. Be a good boy.

It is getting late, and in the soft whispering of the night wind, I hear your voice saying the things I long so much to hear. God bless you.

All My Love,
Mother

P.S. Write soon.

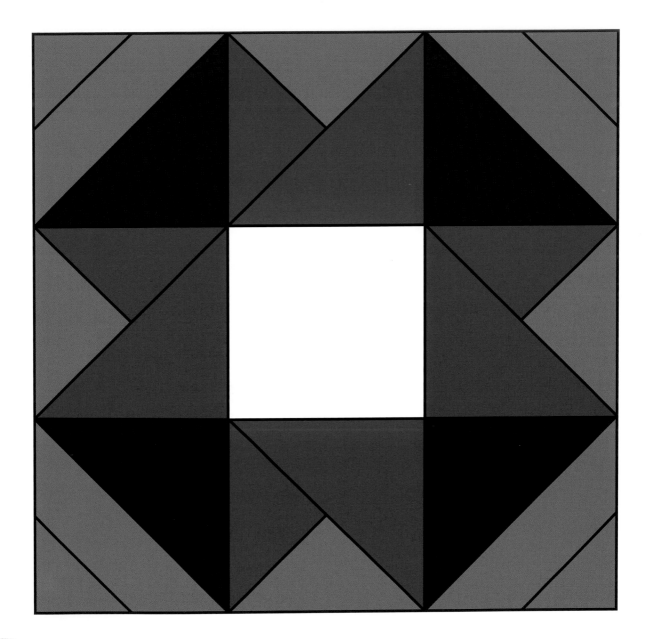

Stephen C. Dvorak

Promise to Your Girlfriend

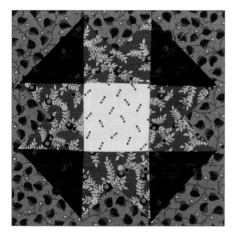

October 1, 1944

Dear Son,

How have you been? I am happy to hear that you received your money on time. The reason I sent the money by telegraph this time was so you would receive it on time. I was working on Tuesday and Wednesday, and about the time I come home from work, the post office closes. I was afraid to send the money as late as Thursday, so I sent it by telegraph to be safe.

I went to Jersey last week. They are all fine and they all send their love. I haven't heard from you in about a week, and I was wondering if you are angry because I asked you not to promise to your girlfriend until the war is over. Anyhow, I missed your letter last week, but I know that you are so busy that you don't have too much time to write to me.

You've been telling me for a long time now about the enjoyable weekends that you have. So I thought I'd tell you about my weekend. On Friday, I saw a good movie, *Since You Went Away*. It was a very nice picture and was a lovely story. I enjoyed myself very much. Thursday morning I went to a church service. At dinner I had a delicious fried chicken at the Chinese restaurant. After dinner I went on a bus ride.

All My Love,
Mother

248

Stephen C. Dvorak

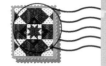

Drink Only Coca-Cola

October 6, 1944

Dear Son,

Thank you very much for your sweet letter. I love to read about your weekend dates. Really, I don't mind at all. I enjoy reading letters about your dates and your girlfriend very much. I'm anxious to hear a little bit more about Barbara.

My little boy, please drink only Coca-Cola. You know your mother worries about you horribly. Today I sent you a box, and in it I put a rum fruitcake, cookies and candy. I hope you enjoy them. Don't forget to let me know when it arrives. I sent the package by special delivery, so please let me know how many days it takes to get there.

I received a letter from Anna today. She asked about you, so why don't you write her. How are you feeling these days? I often am thinking of you. Write soon. God bless you.

With All My Love,
Mother

Stephen C. Dvorak

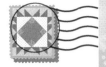

Upset Me Horribly

November 4, 1944

My Dear Son,

I received your letter and was disappointed to read that you would not be home. I felt blue and I was a little sick over you changing your furlough. What does the Army mean, a few more months to wait for your furlough? It is very likely you will not be home for Christmas or New Year's if I'm right. Soon it will be Thanksgiving.

I'd like to send you cookies, and I'd like to know if you want me to send a pair of gloves with the cookies. Please be sure to let me know soon.

I'm sorry I am not able to write you a long letter now, it seems that something happened with me. I suppose it's because you can't come home, it upset me horribly. But when night comes, I will open up our prayer book to pray for you always. Be a good boy. Take care of yourself. Write soon. God bless you my dear son.

Love,
Mother

Stephen C. Dvorak

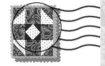

A Comfort to Me

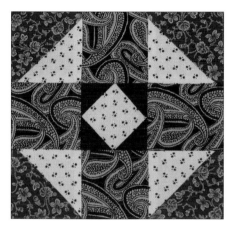

December 11, 1944

My Dear Son,

Just a few lines hoping to find you in the best of health. Another week has rolled by. Soon it will be Christmas, and I'm wondering if you're coming home. Before I go any further, you better know that you don't have to worry about returning the money. When you come home, I will tell you all about the story of why you don't have to return the money to me. If you make any profit, it is all yours. I hope you are satisfied now.

You always wanted to buy a car and you have now. I want you to have a good time and enjoy yourself while you have your car. I did answer your friend's letter, and I asked him in case he is here the following Sunday, if he would stop and have a visit with me. Yes, I still see Madeline. She came for supper, you know everybody likes your mother's cooking.

Thank you for your lovely letter. It makes me very happy to know that I have a lovely and dearest son, a true friend who has always been such a comfort to me. I won't write much more to you today, but I have so many things I want to talk about when you come home. I ask the Lord every night to guide you and watch over you. Take good care of yourself. Write soon. God bless you.

All My Love,
Mother

Stephen C. Dvorak

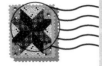

Which Sailboat

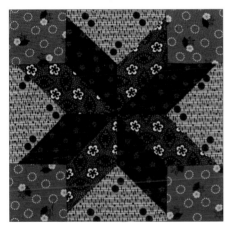

January 21, 1945

My Dear Son,

Just a few lines hoping to find you in the best of health. I received your letter and money order, thank you so very much. Before I go any further, please explain to me why you did not cash the money order? I'm glad to hear that you had a grand dinner on your birthday because as long as you can't be home, I can't treat you to a birthday dinner. That made me feel good to know that people treat you so well.

Tell me which sailboat you want me to send to your friend. Did Anna send you a birthday card? I know there is not much to be against, I just think those who love each other try to be together.

I am sure that you will be feeling better after the operation. Please let me know, and if it is all right, I will send you the apricot cake. Be sure to let me know when. Take good care of yourself. I wonder if you have received the letter I wrote you last week. Write soon. God bless you my dear son.

Love,
Mother

Stephen C. Dvorak

256

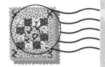

January 28, 1945

Apricot Jam

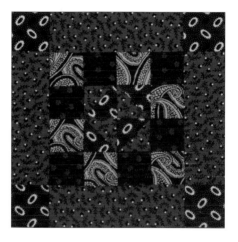

My Dear Son,

Thank you very much for your very lovely letter. I can assure you I had a very pleasant hour or so reading your sweet letter. Sometimes I think my silly letters make you very tired to read. I'm so glad you're feeling fine. When you leave the hospital, please take good care of yourself.

I very much enjoyed reading your letter about your girlfriend. It is nice to have a friend; a true friend is a very rare thing in this world. If she likes you and you like her, that's the important thing. She must be a pretty girl. I am very happy you have such a nice girlfriend and that her mother is also nice to you and feeds you roast chicken and homemade noodles. It must be wonderful. When you go there, be a nice boy.

I mailed you a sailboat on January 27th. I packed it very carefully. I hope you got it safely. The package cost $0.80 with insurance. Saturday I went shopping and found I could get two pounds of brown sugar and three pounds of granulated sugar, so I made four quarts of apricot jam.

Everything is just about the same except the weather. We will have a cold winter this year.

Give my regards to your friends in Pittsburgh. Please let me hear from you soon. God bless you.

Forever Loving,
Mother

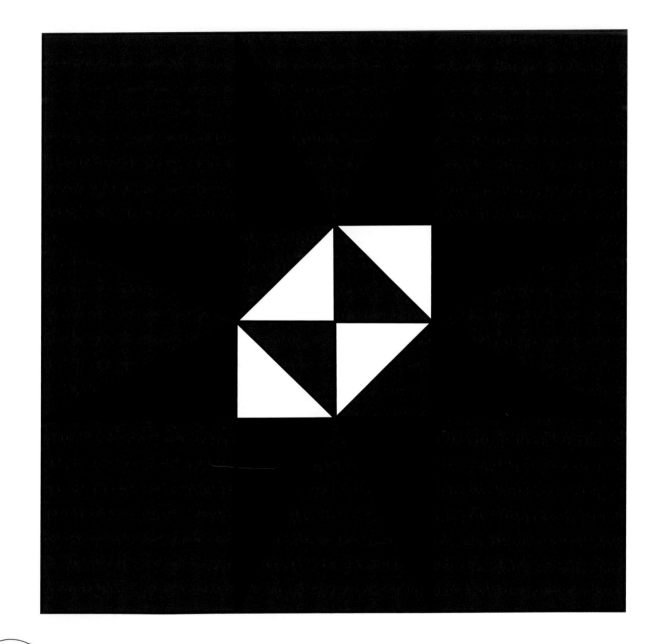

Stephen C. Dvorak

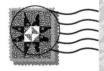

The World Seemed Bright

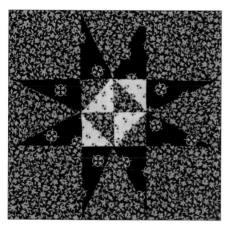

February 7, 1945

My Dear Son,

   Indeed I was surprised to hear you have been discharged from the hospital so soon. Tell me you are all right. How long were you in the hospital? I would like to know if the boat arrived safely and not broken up in small pieces.

   Last night I had a dream. I dreamed the war was over and you came home. That news will mean a lot to me. In the moment when I woke up, all the world seemed bright, but it was only a pleasant dream. I hope my dream comes true soon. Do you remember a year ago when you were home? Yes, it has been a long time since you've been home. I am hoping that you will soon begin to return home.

   Anna must be very angry with you if she didn't send you a birthday card. I don't think she is angry because you didn't thank her for the Christmas present, I think it is something else. She has no reason to be angry. You should not worry about it now.

   The cold weather didn't bother me very much. I think that spring is around the corner and I hope I will feel better when the nice weather comes. Please let me know when you would like to have the cookies sent to you. Take good care of yourself. Write soon. God bless you.

                    All My Love,
                    Mother

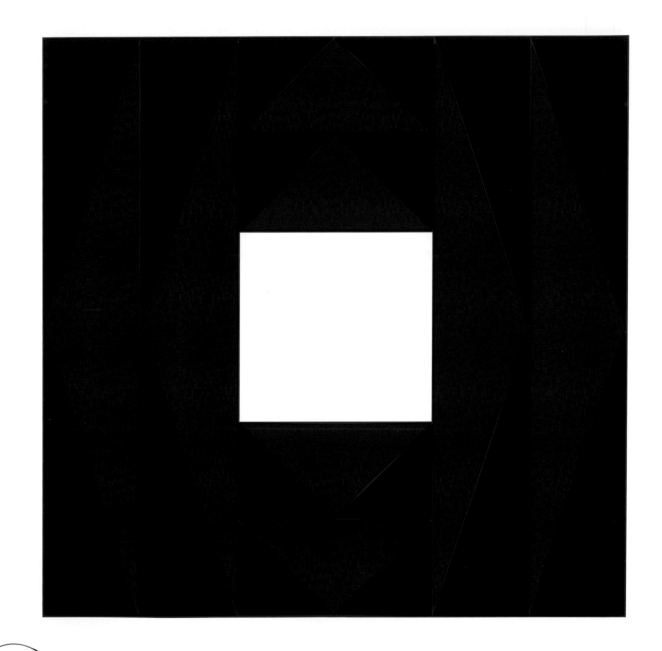

Stephen C. Dvorak

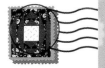

No Meat

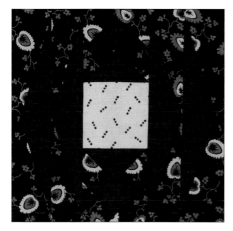

February 12, 1945

My Dear Son,

Today is Sunday and, of course, I'm reading my Sunday paper, trying to read the news about the war. At this moment, everyone is wondering how long the war will last. No one knows, but one of these days the war will be over. I hope for and I think of the time when we shall be together again. Sunday was a very lonely day for me.

I thank you 1,000 times for the sugar. My Sunday chicken dinner disappeared from the table. Last week I had no meat. This week I have support because I have no meat every week. I don't worry about it, we have plenty of other things to eat.

Last Wednesday, I saw a good show, *A Song to Remember*. It was about the great Polish pianist and composer Frederick Chopin. It was different from any picture that I have ever seen before, with beautiful melodies. It was swell and I enjoyed myself very much.

Write soon. Take good care of yourself. I pray for you always. God bless you.

With Lots of Love to You,
Mother

Stephen C. Dvorak

February 20, 1945

National Velvet

My Dear Son,

How have you been? You can hardly imagine how glad I was when I received your letter about the swell time you had sailing your boat. I'd like to be there with you and Elizabeth. Thank you for a lovely Valentine card.

Yes, I do remember the old lady's grandson, I used to see him when he used to come to see the old lady. Do you remember the Morrissey family? This Thursday morning she died. The mother was very fond of her son, and it was just too much for her to lose a son. She died and on Sunday morning, the father was taken to the hospital, it was very sad.

I have not heard anything about whether or not you'd like to have some homemade cookies. If you wish, please let me know, my little boy.

Sunday I went to a church service and in the afternoon I went to see National Velvet. It was a lovely story, I enjoyed the picture very much.

Let me know if you get mail from Henry and from little Helen. Hoping to hear from you soon. Be a good boy. Take care of yourself.

My Love and Blessings,
Your Loving Mother

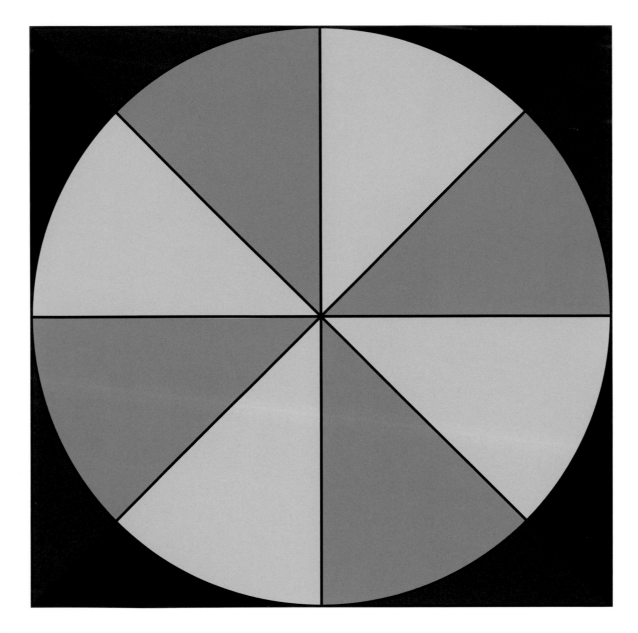

Stephen C. Dvorak

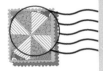

March 18, 1945

Your Engagement

My Dear Son,

I was surprised at receiving your letter yesterday morning, but not unpleasantly. Heard the news about your engagement with Elizabeth in a month or two. Anyways, I am pretty upset about all that. I asked you 1,000 times not to engage your promise while you are in the Army. You are going to hurt yourself, not me. You have no money to buy a ring and you think you're going to be getting engaged to Elizabeth? I have not a thing to say anymore, do what you please. I am not angry with you because you're getting engaged, you are still my little boy blue.

Let me know when you want the money. I can send you $100. Please do not ask Anna for money, I told you last time not to ask Anna. What a silly thing you are telling me about, when you marry I should live in the same house with you. Let's not talk about it now. When the time comes, that will be another story.

I have faith and I believe in God, and God takes care of me. But when night comes, I can open the memory book to think about yesterday, our dream, a dream about you. I wish you the best of luck.

Be a good boy. Take good care of yourself. Give my regards to your friends in Pittsburgh. Write soon. I pray for you always. God bless you.

Love,
Mother

Stephen C. Dvorak

April 4, 1945

Deep Interest

My Dear Son,

I am sorry to hear the bad news about your happiness. I understand how you feel about Elizabeth. I like her very much and you can tell her that. She is a very sweet little girl. I don't blame her parents for being careful about who should be their son-in-law. They are worried about her. One thing I'll ask you: Try not to see her every week. I know you think the world of her, but when you finish your schooling, her parents will be open to meeting you again. You are only 23 years old, and your life has only begun. Life is a funny affair.

Did you have a nice Easter? I spent Easter Sunday in bed. There is nothing that can comfort me anymore. I attended the Good Friday communion service at 8 p.m. and planned to attend the Sunrise Service for the first time in my life. Unfortunately, my dream did not come true.

I mailed you some cameras today. I sent two. I didn't know which one you wanted. I sent some candy and cookies, too.

Dearest, believe that I have the deepest interest in your love affairs and desire to share your joys and sorrows alike. Write soon. Be a good boy. Take good care of yourself.

All My Love,
Mother

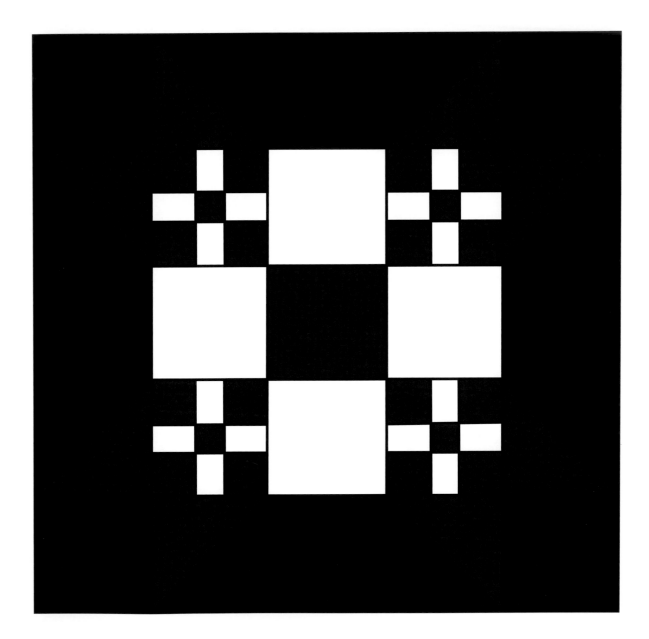

268

Stephen C. Dvorak

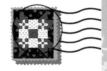

May 1, 1945

My Dearest Son,

Another month has rolled by, time sure goes by fast. Today is May 1st, and it has been raining all day. How is the weather at Camp Crowder? You have been telling me about the good times when you leave on Sundays. I am very glad to hear that. Yesterday I was at Mary's and I sent a luncheon invitation to Elizabeth's mother. I wrote a short note, something like this:

Dear Mrs. Drenik,
I would like to thank you for the lovely time Stephen has had every Sunday. I hope that I'll be able to return it. Thank you again for being so wonderful to my boy.

Please let me know if the note was all right. I hope that Mrs. Drenik would like to come to the luncheon. I had to send Elizabeth's mother something because you go there every Sunday and she feeds you so well. So, this way, I can return the favor and send an invitation to Mrs. Drenik. I think the people in Pittsburgh are wonderful to the boys. You don't find kindhearted people in New York.

Monday I saw A Tree Grows in Brooklyn and it was swell. The Enchanted Cottage is going to come to the Coliseum and I hope to go see it. I have been wondering if you have received a letter from Henry. Let me know.

Take good care of yourself, write soon. Give my regards to your friends in Pittsburgh. God bless you.

Lots of Love to You,
Mother

An Invitation

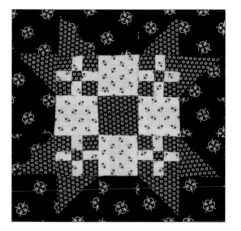

Stephen C. Dvorak

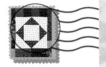

June 21, 1945

Hope

My Dear Son,

The last few days we have had very warm weather. Sunday the temperature was 90 degrees. I have so many things I want to write about, but I have not been in a mood to write. I received your nice letters. I have never enjoyed anything so much as reading your letters.

I think the Bill of Rights is wonderful, it will help you finish your schooling. Yes, the last group of photographs you sent, I liked all of them the best. Thank you so very much.

I see you are still in love with Elizabeth. You know something, they say that love is blind. Of course, I dare not say all this to you, I must not do anything to hurt your feelings. I wonder if Elizabeth cares as much for you as you care for her.

Yes, I see Bob's grandmother sometimes. I thank you 1,000 times for the ration stamps. June 6th I sent you a box of Loft's Candy and I hope that you enjoy them. It is two weeks ago that I sent the candy. I hope you have received it by now, please let me know.

I mailed you $15 today. I had a very pleasant sail up the Hudson by myself on Monday. I hope my dreams come true and my next trip up the Hudson will be with you.

Write soon. Take good care of yourself. I pray for you always. God bless you.

All My Love,
Mother

Meet the Quilters

I would like to thank my special group of quilting friends, each of whom made nine blocks for the World War II quilt. Working with these friends made the project that much more exciting, and it was definitely interesting to see the color choices that each quilter made. I encourage any guild or quilting group to get together and use these patterns for raffle quilts or special gifts. Quilting together certainly makes the process more fun!

Front row: Jeanne Meddaugh , Rosemary Youngs, Barbara Perrin. Second row: Gay Bomers, Elaine Frey , Karen Weilder, Connie Makl, Patty Harrants, Janis Nelson and Carla Jolman.

About the Author

Rosemary Youngs has been quilting since the 1980s. Her quilts have won numerous awards in local as well as major shows. Pictures of her work have been published in various books and magazines. She has taught at local shops and enjoys designing quilts that tell stories. Her first book, *The Amish Circle Quilt*, published in 2004, tells the story of 11 Amish women, their culture and quilting. Her other books include *The Civil War Diary Quilt*, *The Civil War Love Letter Quilt*, and *The Civil War Anniversary Quilt*.